Hidden Mountain,

Secret Garden

Dr. Anthony Lilles has authored an introduction to prayer that is inspiring and encouraging. For those desiring to pray this is a resource that is full of practical advice – written simply and attractively. This book bears the mark of a man – husband, father and teacher – who is not only imbued with the wisdom of the Saints, but who has also, through his own prayer, learned how all of us can, through prayer, foster faith in and love for Jesus and his Gospel.

THOMAS G. WEINANDY, O.F.M., CAP.
Executive Director for the Secretariat for Doctrine
United States Conference of Catholic Bishops

This is a wonderful book. I've taught spiritual theology many years and I wish I had had this text use. In fact, I wish I had written this book. It is scriptural, patristic, historical, theological, mystical, experiential and user friendly. Dr. Lilles takes us through the spiritual journey of prayer, citing Fathers and doctors, saints and even sinners to guide us on our Christian way toward contemplation. Weaving many themes into a harmonious whole, he opens up the life of contemplation for all Christians, our baptismal birthright in a way that is accessible and attractive. This is a book one will read more than once.

FR. GILES DIMOCK, O.P., S.T.D
University Parish of St. Thomas Aquinas
At the University of Virginia

In this book we find the real meat of the new evangelization. The church in America will not be renewed by "facts about Jesus" but only through one's choice to let Christ reach the heart and change it from within. It is an ancient message received by only few: Do not be afraid of letting go of what now defines you. Let Christ *tell you who you are*. Dr. Lilles is one of the ablest guides to lead us through to such a choice. Will I stay with knowledge about Jesus or will I enter the garden of prayer and finally come to know Him!! Do not be afraid to be loved, read this book.

DEACON JAMES KEATING, PH.D,
Institute for Priestly Formation, Omaha, NE

"Jesus is the revelation of God's thirst for humanity" (p.19) with these words Anthony Lilles gives us the key to prayer. In *Hidden Mountain, Secret Garden*, we are shown the key to the most important thing in life. We were made by Love, and we were made for Love, but a thousand things seem to distract us from the one thing most needed; a personal encounter with Jesus Christ. The good news... No, the great news is that Jesus desires a relationship with us even more than we desire one with Him, and He alone is able to overcome our distractions and lead us to become the men and women we were meant to be.

CURTIS MARTIN
President & Founder FOCUS

In every chapter of this book, Anthony, with an unusual skill and insight in our day, with Christ, leads us to this great feast. Anthony has accomplished a rare feat in providing deep theological and heart reflection on prayer that will appeal to both seasoned pilgrims, and those who are just beginning their journey. If you are looking for an easy path to assuage your restless heart, this is not the place to look. But, if you are ready to dig deep and explore the reality of what it means to engage with God and enter into what St. Teresa of Avila called the Interior Castle, this is one of the best places I know to start. Anthony will not only get you over the moat into the Castle, he will also prove a sure guide to your journey and your destiny, deep into the heart of God.

DAN BURKE
Executive Director of the National Catholic Register
Author of Navigating the Interior Life, Spiritual Direction and the Journey to God

Hidden Mountain, Secret Garden

A Theological Contemplation On Prayer

Anthony Lilles

Discerning Hearts
Omaha, Nebraska

Discerning Hearts
Omaha, Nebraska
www.discerninghearts.com

ISBN-13: 978-0988627000 (Discerning Hearts)
ISBN-10: 0988627000

Dedication
To my brothers – by blood, marriage and faith
Forsake not the discipline.

Thursday, November 8, 2012
Feast of Blessed Elisabeth of the Trinity

Acknowledgements

Unto the Praise of Glory!
A couple of decades ago, on a beautiful Roman day, a Dominican and a Jesuit walked down from Santa Sabina to the Tiber in deep discussion about the renewal of the Church. I was following, and still am. Father Giles Dimock, O.P., a spiritual father, friend and my professor at Franciscan University of Steubenville as well as the Angelicum, provided theological and spiritual guidance which helped me see the hidden mountain and secret garden of prayer. Father Raymond Gawronski, S.J., reviewed this book for doctrinal integrity as censor for the Archdiocese of Denver. Also a friend and spiritual father, those familiar with his work Word and Silence will find its influence in these pages.

In addition to the generosity of the Archdiocese of Denver and St. John Vianney Theological Seminary which made this project possible, I am also grateful to Dan Burke, Deacon Jim Keating, and Father Timothy Gallagher for their solid counsel. A debt of gratitude is also owed to Marc Lenzini and Celeste Thomas whose editing skills are outmatched only by their devotion to the Lord. Special acknowledgement goes to Ann Phillips, the artist who provided the cover art. Finally, this book would not be in your hands without Kris McGregor of Discerning Hearts, a pioneer in the new media, who was inspired to start a publishing house so that works like this might be available to you.

Table of Contents

INTRODUCTION

*He who climbs never stops going from beginning to beginning,
through beginnings that have no end. He never stops desiring
what he already knows.*
St. Gregory of Nyssa[1]

The great Christians who have gone before us are like
mountaineers. In very high altitudes, climbers do not distract
themselves with what they have already done or how much further they must go. Instead, as if beginning for the first time, they
focus only on their next step. It is the only way to reach the summit.

Similarly, in the effort to raise our minds to the Lord, the
saints help us see that each day brings its own challenge. Their
holiness testifies that we must constantly renew our effort to pray
if we are to enter into the secret of the Lord's heart. Their victo-
ries reveal that the more we climb through these new beginnings,
the deeper our devotion grows and the greater our friendship becomes.

Prayer seeks a hidden mountain; it searches out a secret
garden. The mountain is the presence of the Lord. The garden is
friendship with Him. The prize is priceless. In this quest, no sacrifice is too costly. To make this journey is the reason we were
made.

The saints reveal that this is no one sided quest. No matter how inadequate we feel and no matter how many times we
have failed, their witness tells us that we can begin to pray anew

---

[1] *Hom. In Cant. 8*: PG 44, 941C as translated in the *Catechism of the Catholic
Church*, #2015.

1

because the Lord never abandons us. When we raise our minds to the Living God, He establishes us in the depths of His Heart. If He asks for our humble faith, it is because He comes in divine humility to invite us into the paradise He fashioned by His suffering and death – a heaven that can begin even in the present moment.

Everything there is to know about prayer is already revealed in the Holy Bible and in the tradition of the Church. Yet, through the centuries, Christians have encouraged one another also with their own words. This is because the Lord expects us to help one another along the way. To this end, the following pages present the wisdom of those who have gone before us in the faith.

The Voice of a Prophet

Disturbed by a lecture on Christianity, a young atheist began to read the Gospel of Mark. He had no conscious desire to pray or find God. His intention was the opposite. He was looking to discredit the claims of the Gospel, to show that what it proposed was naïve fantasy.

Having had to flee his home in the midst of violence, this teenage Russian with distinguished family background, had recently relocated to Paris in the 1930s. In his life as a refugee, he found existence to be both bitter and senseless. In fact, prior to a disturbing lecture earlier that evening, Andre Borisovich Bloom had already resolved to kill himself. Invalidating the claims of that evening's speaker would be among his final tasks.[2]

The speaker, an Orthodox priest, had raised a vexing question for the young atheist. Namely, in the face of all the evidence to the contrary, in the face of his life experience, what if the Chris-

---

[2] Father Benedict Groeschel c.f.r. retells this story in *I am with You Always: A study of the History and Meaning of Personal Devotion to Jesus Christ for Catholic, Orthodox, and Protestant Christians*, San Francisco: Ignatius Press (2010), 509ff.

tian proposal was true? In the face of his decision for death, the young man could not ignore this proposal.

Then, the most unexpected encounter changed everything for him. He was reading only the very first chapters of the Gospel of Mark when he became aware of a gentle and peaceful personal presence. His sense of this invisible presence was not a result of the words he read moving him one way or another. But while he read, this mysterious *Someone* continued to disclose Himself to him. In the face of his own bitter judgments, this *Someone* was not condemning, but patiently waiting. Amazement seized him when he connected this spiritual presence with Jesus Christ, the Son of God, the very one about whom the Gospel of Mark bears witness. He was encountering Jesus personally present and truly concerned about him.

The invitation of this Holy Presence of God changed everything for him. He needed to respond. So while he read, he began to pray and as he prayed, he discovered that the deepest human purpose, the thing that most made sense in life, in his life, in every life, had the form of friendship; friendship with God.

This discovery was something he kept alive and fresh in his heart through prayer. His prayer turned into an ongoing conversation with God, an interior dialogue where he opened his heart to the questions posed by this new silent Presence in his life. He came to see that answering these questions involved a whole change of life, a new way of living, a manner of life he had to begin again every day.

Friendship with God, the life of prayer, became the great pursuit of his life. In his faithfulness to this pursuit, he first became a monk and eventually a bishop in the Orthodox Church. Archbishop Bloom understood that his encounter with Christ spoke to a deep spiritual need in our time. People were forgetting how to pray, and they needed someone to remind them of the truth of Christian prayer, someone who would help them make a good beginning.

To this end, Metropolitan Anthony Bloom wrote *Beginning to Pray*. I discovered this delightful book at a summer camp bookstore in the late 70s. I was always aware of the Lord's presence from early childhood. My devotion to Christ, however, was not constant. Faithfully responding to His mysterious love challenged me. Through his provocative use of the Scriptures, the Metropolitan helped me understand that new beginnings are always possible. This book attempts to take up his message again for our own time so that those who feel drawn to prayer might also make a new beginning.

A New Beginning for the Third Millennium

At the dawn of the Third Millennium, it is time to make a new beginning. I am writing because I believe if we take up this new beginning, if we find the hidden mountain and enter the secret garden, not only will our own lives be changed; but also God will do something beautiful in the world. This is why Christians pray. We believe that our prayer makes a real difference for ourselves and for those we love – even for our enemies. For this hope to be realized, however, our effort to make a new beginning in prayer needs to be rooted in the truth.

This contemplation of beginning to pray is written for those of us who are left disappointed with the empty promises of our dazzling culture. Instead of being lifted up to greater authenticity, we find ourselves weighed down by a culture of death. Instead of progress in real social solidarity and mutual concern, we find ourselves increasingly alienated from our neighbors. Instead of finding true standards by which we can objectively discern our lives and communities, we are left frustrated by the hollow cultural myths promoted in the latest news cycle. Here, against these trends, the possibility of prayer presents itself. But here we also come against a difficult riddle: how do we root our effort to begin a life of prayer in the truth?

Many want to see new life in the Church, but they are not sure where to get it. There is a lack of confidence in the rich treasury of prayer we have received. Instead, recourse is made to the latest spiritual fad. To introduce the theme of this work, it is important to offer a short critique regarding these fads against the beautiful things God is doing in our times, the remarkable work He invites us to share in.

The Failure of Fads

Though packaging of each fad is different, the promises of these empty cisterns are old. Always wrapped in the latest psychological theory and politically correct social agenda, these spiritual or religious programs can seduce even the most competent. These packages of techniques and methods are carefully marketed with promises to satisfy our needs for social solidarity, a sense of control and spiritual experience. Yet, even when the promises come to pass, the results are always skewed. They never provide the salvation they promise.

A good beginning to pray must aim at more than a social feeling or a psychological need or an experience. To flourish, the human spirit needs something more than the products of someone's cleverness. Men and women need a ground to stand on, the ground that only the truth provides. It is precisely because spiritual fads do not provide the full truth that they fail to offer any real support for life. No one has ever become a saint by following one of these fads.

The Word of the Father is the truth we need. Hidden from the wise and revealed to the simple, everything we need in life comes to us through Christ the Lord. Until we root our faith in this Living Word, we will not enjoy the bold confidence the Christian life demands or our brothers and sisters need. Prayer is a response to His invitation to ascend His holy mountain and to enter His sacred garden.

The Spiritual Revolution

There have been important voices calling for a renewal of prayer. Blessed John Paul the Great was emphatic that a radical and widespread return to prayer is essential. His clarion call for a new evangelization went side by side with his call for a renewed interiority. He well understood that only spiritual maturity answers the needs of a culture exhausted in commercial and material pursuits. And, he insisted, the only path to spiritual maturity is through renewing our gaze on the face of Christ in prayer.

Until Pope John Paul II came to Denver in 1993 for World Youth Day, he did not have much reason to be confident that Americans would really respond to his call. Indeed, like most Europeans, he had only heard discouraging things about the Church in the United States. Even in America, in Denver itself, there was vehement skepticism that anything good could come from the religious event. In fact, everyone assumed the opposite.

Feeding this skepticism, a terrible wave of brutal gang violence swept through Denver's teenage and young adult communities. In the weeks before World Youth Day, the summer was dubbed "The Summer of Violence."

In the middle of August, however, this narrative was turned upside down. The Pope, Denver and the world experienced a moment of actual grace. With pilgrims coming from all over the world and the Holy Father's arrival, it was as if a whole new presence of Christ settled into the city.

The local response was authentic and from the heart. People were moved to extend generous hospitality in magnificent ways. All over the metro area, people kept stepping forward whether out of curiosity or just a desire to be part of what was going on. Even secular news commentators noted that Denver had dramatically changed, and on occasion they too got caught up in the jubilation. Political leaders and law enforcement officials were astounded to discover, with the inflow of young people from around the world, both violent crime and petty theft significantly decreased. A profound sense of real solidarity permeated the Mile High City.

What followed may be one of the most prayerful gatherings in the history of the United States. Hundreds of thousands of young people from across the United States and around the world walked, talked, sang and prayed along Cherry Creek. On a pilgrimage from lower downtown all the way to an all-night prayer vigil at Cherry Creek State Park, their faith was contagious. The event ended with Mass Sunday morning.

After making a private retreat high in the Rocky Mountains, the Holy Father joined the pilgrims in prayer during the vigil. Some of the pilgrims were overcome with exhaustion, but no one wanted to leave. There was a special bond between the youth and the Holy Father. The explanation for this is simple: true prayer deepens friendship and overcomes every form of social alienation. Fittingly, the theme song for the event was *We Are One Body*.

At the heart of this gathering was a very special encounter with the Lord, an encounter not unlike that which was experienced by Anthony Bloom so many years before. In both instances, the encounter culminated in action. Genuine prayer always leads to a converted life; a life lived for love.

Inviting the pilgrims to boldly proclaim the Gospel "from the rooftops" of the modern metropolis, the Pope also encouraged the young people of the world not to fear a life-changing encounter with Christ. Jesus, he insisted, was the only answer to the deepest needs of the human heart. By our dedication to a close relationship with Him, the Pope insisted that we could build a culture of life and civilization of love, repeating, "Be proud of the Gospel of Christ!"

If these words resonated in the hearts of those who were there, it is because in some way they felt the presence of Christ with them. Many participants, even non-Christians, left with the desire to enter more deeply into prayer, to seek the Living God. As for the Pope, he came to see this as an extraordinary grace, a history changing moment. For years afterward, when Denver was mentioned to him, Blessed John Paul II would exclaim, *"Revolution!"*

A spiritual revival began to take hold. It was as if new life returned to a patient many had already given up for dead, and this new life was contagious. Nationally, Catholic media efforts, like *Eternal Word Television Network*, were injected with a renewed sense of vigor and purpose. Young people began to look at the priesthood and religious life in a new way. Movements like *Youth 2000* gained new momentum. The religious sensibility of America had been touched.

What happened to the Revolution?

The spiritual revolution identified by John Paul II found concrete expression in the generous decisions of heroic young people to offer their lives to God in a variety of beautiful ways. This included renewed interest in the priesthood. To respond, the Archdiocese of Denver founded St. John Vianney Theological Seminary. From its inception, this institution has been permeated with a new emphasis on the primacy of prayer that the Pilgrim Pope helped us discover.

The grace of World Youth Day converged with other efforts in the Church at the time. In the years prior to founding the new seminary, Church documents, partly in an attempt to address the large number of newly ordained priests leaving the ministry, called for a year of prayer and catechesis to be introduced prior to formal study.[3]

---

[3] For example, *Pastores Dabo Vobis*, 62. This was written just the year before World Youth Day '93 and about seven years before the opening of St. John Vianney Theological Seminary. To the great benefit of St. John Vianney Theological Seminary, there were many attempts to address the concerns raised by

Introduction

Seminarians needed more than better catechesis or even familiarity with basic spiritual practices; they needed a whole new way of life flowing from an encounter with Christ. In other words, there was a conviction that the restoration of the priesthood and the Church would require a renewed dedication to ongoing conversion, the kind that can only emerge through serious engagement in contemplative mental prayer. Our tradition identifies such a way of life as a *conversatio morum* – putting one's whole life in conversation with the Risen Lord.[4]

Although very few bishops felt the need to add another year to priestly formation, Archbishop Francis Stafford (now Cardinal) and his successor, Archbishop Charles Chaput, O.F.M.Cap. (now Archbishop of Philadelphia), understood that seminarians needed deeper spiritual grounding in Christ. To this end, as the opportunity to begin this new work presented itself, Archbishop Chaput tasked Father Samuel Aquila, the eventual Archbishop of Denver, with proposing a new model for a seminary.

Involved in helping to host World Youth Day, the then Father Aquila understood the importance of a genuine encounter of Christ in the life of faith. Rather than imitating conventional practices, his considered new bold efforts taken up in Philadelphia and in Paris. Both places brought prayer and doctrine to bear in seminary life in original and effective ways.

Contributing to this discernment, a very important meeting took place in a monastery in a remote part of Northern California. For those who have not been to Mount Tabor in Ukiah, try to imagine onion shaped domes and wooden stave architecture

---

John Paul II in this document, including a symposium in Paris. Today, however, very few seminaries have anything like a Spirituality Year experience. Given the successes realized in Denver, this is a surprising outcome.

[4] *Conversatio morum* is a commitment to ongoing examination and conversion of the whole manner of one's daily life in light of the Gospel of Christ. This commitment is a way of life taken up by monks, religious, and other ascetics, especially the Benedictines. To translate this as a simple change of behavior misses the mark. See *The Rule of St. Benedict*, #58.

sheltered by rolling hills and forest. The chapel is filled with incense and icons, and echoes with the mysterious beauty of Byzantine chants. It is a sacred place where many have gone to encounter the Living God.

It was at this holy mountain that Father John Hilton met with Father Raymond Gawronski, S.J. Father Hilton, a well-loved pastor noted for his life of prayer, had experience working with young men in vocational discernment for Denver. Father Gawronski, a Byzantine Catholic monk and tenured Jesuit professor from Marquette at the time, had dedicated his life to advance what he called *a kneeling theology*; the kind of prayerful study aimed at building up the holiness of the Church. Both had shared the experience of World Youth Day. Together, immersed in prayer, they discussed a new kind of contemplative intellectuality that priests of the Third Millennium would need to engage.

Through these discussions and the discernment that followed, the Church in Denver was able to give birth to a renewed vision for priestly formation. This vision unfolded on the conviction that only an ongoing encounter with Christ in prayer could serve as the authentic source of a seminarian's *conversatio morum*; his ongoing conversion to a life lived for love of God and neighbor. The men would be taught from the beginning that taking up the standard of Christ involves a surrender of one's whole existence, including in the way they think about themselves and see the world.

The fruit of this discernment is the new seminary enjoyed and generously supported by the Archdiocese of Denver today. Offering seven years of rigorous formation, special emphasis is given to the spiritual life. Seminarians dedicate a whole year to contemplative prayer and engage in a variety of apostolic projects before taking up philosophical and theological studies. This Spirituality Year ends with the *Spiritual Exercises* of St. Ignatius given in a guided retreat for thirty days.

Introduction

This intense encounter with Christ is followed up on throughout the rest of their formation with ongoing spiritual direction, prayerful reading of the Scriptures in small groups called *Lectio Divina*, and annual retreats. A genuine effort to build a communion of friendship in Christ animates the community. Additionally, new cohorts of future clergy advancing through this intense formation find support in a whole team of wonderful spiritual directors, confessors, preachers, other advisors and a very dedicated academic faculty.

This effort to put prayer first is a work in progress, one bearing good fruit. Although often thrown into extremely difficult pastoral situations very early after their ordinations, our new priests have a solid spiritual foundation that will bless the Church for years to come. The spiritual revolution Blessed John Paul II started in Denver towards the end of the Second Millennium is being passed on to a new generation.

This book derives from lectures given to these seminarians. The material was developed specifically for the Spirituality Year over a twelve-year period. Aimed at introducing the spiritual life through a meditative reading of the great classics of the Catholic Spiritual tradition, it has often occurred to me that some of what the men share together would be helpful not only in formation for the priesthood, but for anyone trying to begin a life of prayer.

The spiritual revolution of Blessed John Paul II, the mysterious presence encountered by Metropolitan Bloom, and our own need to make a new beginning all converge on the Gospel of Christ. We will see that our tradition has understood faith in Christ with images like a hidden mountain and a secret garden. There are powerful insights in these traditional teachings that can help us make a new beginning.

Those To Whom this Work is Offered

The following pages are intended especially for those who are looking for answers about life and about their relationship with God. The uncertainty surrounding these questions drove Anthony Bloom to read the Gospel and these are the very same concerns that came alive in Denver during World Youth Day. The best books do not try to explain such painful riddles but instead humbly point to the *Answer* that animates them. We have attempted to accomplish this here.

One voice not often heard by those wrestling with such questions is that which emerges from the contemplative dimension of the Church. This is specifically the voice of the saints, canonized or not. They also had to deal with these same riddles. To this end, they dedicated their lives to listening to the Father's answer, the Word made flesh. Their wisdom is an important signpost to reassure us on our way as we follow this same answer where He leads.

The saints and great contemplatives witness to heights and depths that reach beyond the horizons of this earthly existence and yet allow this present life to brim with both jubilation and holy sorrow. The world in which they lived was no obstacle to this pursuit. If they entered into the concerns of the society in which they lived, they entered even deeper into the hearts of those who were marginalized by it. Their prayer blazed a pathway *in this world* but not *of it*. Not indifferent nor disengaged, not anxious nor enchanted, in the face of cultural and political powers, they speak of a kind of prayer directed deep into the riddle of life that implicates us all.

Those who seek the Lord in this kind of prayer want to open themselves generously to those hidden purposes He has for us. To embark on this journey is to choose to be vulnerable to the true greatness written into our nature, that greatness hidden in the concrete here and now of day-to-day existence. The hidden mountain and secret garden is, therefore, not a search for the esoteric, but a deeper grounding in the present moment.

Not a How-to Book on Prayer

Many, in approaching a book like this, would prefer a "how-to" manual. I do not apologize for not providing such a manual. Prayer is too simple and too human of a reality to treat in this way. Anything done for its own sake, like surfing or enjoying a banquet or falling-in-love, defies such "how-to" explanations. Some things are learned only by doing them.

When my friends took me surfing for the first time, they laughed at all my questions about technique. I was so anxious about getting it right that I was missing the whole point. Finally, after a little teasing, they sent me into the surf with the simple challenge: *go for it.* Likewise, when it comes to prayer, if someone wants to know how to pray, I would counsel: *go for it.* Picking up method is something that comes along the way and, as prayer matures, it is often lost sight of completely before the wonder of the Lord.

Prayer cannot be mastered. It is not a skill. Like the sea, it is an immense, dynamic and humbling reality. Prayer launches into the untamed ocean of God's love. Against this mystery, prayer is not the mastery of some set of magical practices, psychological exercises for good mental hygiene or techniques for achieving psychic states. Prayer in fact cannot be mastered at all, although, through it one does discover how to master oneself.

Prayer is about baptism into the death of Christ and rising up in His new life. Such prayer sets out on an ardent search for the One who searches for me: the heart and mind rising up again and again in this quest even in the face of heartrending disappointment and overwhelming sorrow. Here is where the most intimate conversation with the One who dwells in my innermost self takes place.

Such prayer is a spiritual listening, a mystical gaze, a holy silence and a cry of recognition from the depths of one's being. In the end, there are no tricks to teach, no shortcuts to take. We must surrender our pride and appeal to the mercy of God with humble trust. When this happens, when prayer takes on the proportions of real love (and this is only possible by gift of His mercy in us), something worthy of God is born in the heart. The possibility of true friendship with the Lord is opened up.

The Kind of Prayer this Book Explores

Our plan is to provide a guided tour of the Lord's hidden mountain and secret garden, at least insofar as the Holy Bible and writings of the saints who lived by its teachings allow. It is a tour from the outside looking in for these are places only prayer itself actually enters. This exploration of the wisdom of the saints proposes a kind of map and binoculars for the life of prayer. If a good map and set of binoculars is sometimes useful on a hike, on our spiritual journey, the doctrine of those who have gone before us in the Lord can be indispensable.

In our first chapter we will see the thirst compelling us to take this journey does not self-originating but is caused by a beautiful mystery outside of ourselves. The source of prayer wells up beyond the narrow limits of our own egos. We thirst for Jesus because He first thirsts for us. In Chapter Two, we will consider the collision of doubt and faith into which the waters of prayer baptize us. In our third chapter, we will consider the sign of the Cross under which prayer begins and to which it progresses on this pathway.

Having introduced its source and goal, we then consider how the mystery of prayer unfolds. Through the trials of prayer, God transforms us into His likeness. Just as He is Love, we must learn to love. The fourth, fifth, sixth and seven chapters take up prayer as a lover's quest through dark nights and all kinds of

14

hardship. The Lord's hidden mountain is found by faith alone and ascending it entails fighting great spiritual battles all along the way. In all of this, we will see God's transforming love opening up a spiritual trysting place in our innermost being, the secret garden where we are made fruitful for God.

The final part of this work considers what it means to share in the victory of the Risen Lord. In this secret garden, the greatness of the human spirit is revealed in the compassionate humility that comes from Christ. By prayer, God's love, instead of personal failure, becomes the defining reality of our existence. In our conclusion we will see that prayer is no private pursuit: all of heaven implicates itself in our effort to pray. When we pray, we are in communion with those who have gone before us in the faith. With them, we too realize the triumph of good over evil.

No other kind of prayer is as worth the effort as is the humble movement of Christian prayer. No other kind of prayer addresses our deepest human needs. No other prayer helps us to thrive to the full. Genuine Christian prayer alone offers a real relationship with the Lord in which each of us becomes more fully ourselves the closer we draw to Him. This is why prayer was essential to the project of Blessed John Paul II:

> Is it not one of the "signs of the times" that in today's world, despite widespread secularization, there is *a widespread demand for spirituality*, a demand which expresses itself in large part as *a renewed need for prayer*? ... Christian communities must become *genuine "schools" of prayer*, where the meeting with Christ is expressed not just in imploring help but also in thanksgiving, praise, adoration, contemplation, listening and ardent devotion, until the heart truly "falls in love". [5]

---

[5] Apostolic Letter, *Novo Millenio Ineunte*, January 6, 2001, #33 as translated at www.vatican.va. – Liberia Editrice Vaticana

To truly fall in love with Christ, to engage Him in a real face to face, heart to heart relationship, this is the whole reason the Church exists. It is the whole reason for our faith. It is the deepest purpose of prayer.

Pope Benedict gets to the same idea in his thoughts about seminaries. His reflections really ought to be applied to all Catholic institutions dedicated to the discipline of theology. The purpose of these institutions "is to be a place of encounter with Jesus Christ, which binds people to him in such a way that they are able to become his voice in the present, his voice for the people and the world of today."[6]

Deep prayer is the heartbeat, the life-blood, of the renewal of the Church. The late spiritual theologian Father Jordan Aumann, O.P. insisted that there never has been any true restoration of the Church not preceded by a widespread return to the heights and depths of prayer. Such prayer brings life to the Church and enlivens theology so that it can fulfill its vital role. To this end, Hans Urs von Balthazar is convinced that "only those theologies became vitally effective in history which bore their spirituality not as an addition but within themselves, which embodied it in their innermost being."[7]

Invitation to a Theological Contemplation of Prayer

This exploration intends to be a word of hope, a little encouragement for the journey we are making together. To this end,

---

[6]From an article by Pope Benedict XVI collected in *Ein Neues Lied Des Herrn: Christus und Liturgie in der Gegenwart* (Verlag Herder: Freiburg, 1995), originally was published under the title "Perspektiven der Priesterausbildung heute" in Unser Auftrag: Besinnung auf den priesterlichen Dienst, ed. K. Hillenbrand (Wurzburg, 1990), pp. 11-38, as cited in "Preparation for Priestly Ministry" in *A New Song for the Lord: Faith in Christ and Liturgy Today*, Trans. Martha M. Matesich (Crossroads: New York, 1996), 210.
[7] *Convergences: To the Source of the Christian Mystery*, San Francisco: Ignatius (1969, 1983), p. 44.

we must go beyond simple assertions regarding good practice. Rather, we aim at a theological contemplation of prayer – that is, a vision of prayer as it is in itself.

This work struggles to point to a rich, inexhaustible horizon, filled with wondrous possibilities. We will glimpse into mysteries before which every explanation falls short and no description suffices.

Deep prayer is too vast, too rich, and too beautiful to be adequately explained. Yet I yearn for us to gaze on this horizon together, to feel it tug at our hearts, to let it draw us together into prayer. In this vision, our doubts take their proper place and we find reason for the hope we have within.

The theological understanding of prayer we are looking for is found not only in the truths proposed by our faith themselves, but above all is glimpsed at as something *borne* upon them, like a reflection. Sacred doctrine, prayerfully considered, allows us to glimpse Him, as in a mirror, so that the substance of the truth we believe might pierce our hearts. This was the experience of Anthony Bloom. This was the experience of World Youth Day. This is the ongoing experience of the many men and women who have devoted their lives to searching for and serving the Lord. If we conduct this search well, it should take us, in the end, to what is revealed on the Cross – the true source and summit of our spiritual revolution – the threshold to ever-new "beginnings that have no end."

Chapter One

God's Thirst – the Wellspring of Prayer

Jesus is the revelation of God's thirst for humanity and humanity's thirst of God. This first chapter considers the revelation of prayer in Christ. He is the cause, the pattern and the purpose of Christian prayer. In Christ, God's thirst for us produces our thirst for Him. If the blood and water flowing from his open side make us thirst for more, the overflowing tears of a contrite heart also console the Savior who awaits us in love.

It seems scandalous to speak of God yearning and aching for humanity, but our tradition presents no other kind of God. The Sacred Scriptures speak of Him not only as the Fountain of Life, the One through whom all things came to be; He is also the One who emptied himself, took the form of a slave, humbling Himself unto death. He is the Eternal Word of the Father who for our sake entered into the mortal silence of our flesh. An ancient homily read as part of the Holy Saturday Office of Readings describes Christ, "Greatly desiring to visit those who live in darkness and the shadow of death."

Our search for the Lord in prayer begins because the Almighty God has first gone in search of us. He created us to be in friendship with Him. Seduced into not trusting Him, we have hidden ourselves in a jungle of guilt and shame. So deep is our shame, we are lost in it, unable to find our way out on our own.

There are many who think the Christian teaching about Hell is too severe—that real possibility that, without divine assistance, we could actually enter into a state of perpetual torment forever. This possibility stands to reason, however. People are capable of choosing Hell in the next life because they have already become familiar with it in this life. Sewn into human nature is a kind of ignorance that inclines us to hide in the misery with which we are familiar rather than come out into the open and face God. Perpetual torment however is not why God created humanity.

God's desire for humanity is not that it should be reduced to tormented alienation from itself but that all that is genuinely human should awaken to love. Our faith proposes that humanity was fashioned in the divine image and likeness for a great and noble purpose. To help us realize this divine plan, we profess that before He rose from the dead, Christ descended into hell.

The ancient homily for Holy Saturday quoted above describes Jesus' descent into Hell as a search for the original man and woman, Adam and Eve. He is described as commanding our primordial parents to wake up out of their spiritual slumber. The beatitude for which they were created is totally other than the alienated misery in which Christ finds them. The beatitude they were made for is one of intimate communion and tender love. And, they can rise up out of alienation and leave that torment behind because "You are in me and I am in you, together we form only one person and we cannot be separated."[8]

This description not only helps us ponder the theological reality accomplished in the harrowing of hell, but what happens whenever we allow Christ to enter into our own personal misery through prayer. Just as our tradition suggests Christ went in search for our first parents, we believe He continues to be in search of each of us. He wants to find us, to awaken us to love, to come back with Him to the love in which and for which we were first created.

"Where are you?" This is God's first recorded question to humanity, the question mysteriously posed to Adam and Eve as they hid in shame. The whole Bible could be looked at in terms of God's search for man. If so, the search culminates when the Word becomes flesh. God and man find each other at Golgotha.

---

[8] Anonymous, from *Ancient Homily from Holy Saturday*, in the Office of Readings for Holy Saturday, (PG 43, 439, 451, 462-463).New York: Catholic Book Publishing, 1976.

On the Cross of Christ, all the deepest questions of man and God come together and are revealed in His last whispers and wordless cry. The Lord's cry expresses his thirst. It is both a question and an answer ending in silence. But what kind of silence is it? The Word that poured Himself out for love of us was not vanquished. His silence is not empty or meaningless. The silence of God is pregnant with a love that is stronger than death. It is this love that finds us.

In his undying faithfulness, the Lord has not stopped searching for us. Death could not quench His thirst. He is parched for the water of true friendship with each of us in particular. So passionate is His desire to possess our hearts, He offered His own for us on the Cross. The Lord is able to go any distance and pay any price to win each heart because He has already gone further and paid more than we could ever understand.

Prayer begins in earnest when we hear the Lord's question in our hearts, when we become aware of His thirst, when we allow the silent stillness of his love to envelop us. He thirsts for our friendship. Yet we are not inclined to welcome Him.

Like little children with our hands over our faces, we pretend that if we do not see God, He does not see us. So we close the ear of our hearts to His voice and occupy ourselves with pursuing all kinds of fantasies. We are lost in self-indulgence, insobriety and every form of anxiety – oscillating between despair and hubris. In this way, guilt drives our lives even when we are temporarily successful in our efforts not to feel guilty about our broken existence.

Guilt is so universal an experience that all serious spiritualties propose ways of dealing with it. Christianity identifies sin - our primordial and personal rejection of God - as the cause of guilt. We live in shame because we have sinned against God and ourselves. Part of the greatness of our Catholic faith is that it offers a way to deal with sin so that guilt does not drive our lives.

This is why God has set out to find us. He is actually concerned about our plight. When the Word became flesh God revealed His willingness to enter into our plight, to make our plight His own, so that His goodness and love might become our own.

Christians believe in a saving God who comes to rescue His Beloved from death and hellfire. He comes to raise her up to the dignity of friendship with Him. He comes to lead her home to the place He has prepared for her to dwell with Him forever. No power in heaven or on earth can stop Him. Christian prayer boldly draws all confidence from this.

What is it about humanity that attracts such a Deliverer? He sees in the human being the ineradicable mystery of His image and likeness, an image so beautiful not even sin can blot it out completely. In the holy likeness and divine image with which humanity is endowed, the Image of the Invisible God contemplates the splendor of the Father. His total devotion to the Father permeates all the movements of His soul and unlocks the meaning of everything He said and did. Trusting in his Heavenly Father, He entrusts Himself to us.

As helpless as infant and as defenseless as a condemned man, He continually places Himself in our unworthy hands. He knows our hearts but undaunted comes to us in the disguise of the most vulnerable. It is because of His love for the Father that no matter how much we trust in Him, He has trusted in us even more. His confidence in us is the source and perfection of our confidence in Him. If He has good reason to rely on us, it is because He relies even more on His heavenly Father for everything and searches for the will of His Father in everything.[9] His power is made known in our weakness, His glory in our humiliation, His will in our repentance. And to find Him in these ways is to have life, and to have it to the full.

---

[9] As remarkable as this seems, John Paul II believed that we should have confidence in God because God trusts and has confidence in us. See his address in Toronto for World Youth Day, 2002.

The Prayer of Christ

Traditionally, prayer is called a sacred conversation with God.[10] In this context, the Word made flesh is the crucified question and He is the Risen reply. To encounter Christ the Lord is to allow Him to question our inmost being, to allow God's question to humanity to echo in the vast wilderness of our hearts. Risen and continually sent into our hearts by the Father in the power of the Holy Spirit, the Lord reveals the mystery and discipline of prayer in ever new ways. In the Bible, His prayer is so attractive, His disciples beg Him to teach them to pray like Him. His prayer itself teaches how to pray.[11]

The prayer of the Lord and, by grace, all Christian prayer, is *theandric* – the unity of divine and human activity in his Divine Person. This means, though He is God, when Jesus prays, God prays as man, and though He is man, man prays as God. This is why the Father always hears His prayer and why His prayer raises up the hearts of men. When we join the Risen Lord by faith, the Holy Spirit moves us with the thoughts and affections of the Word made flesh: the prayer of the God-man generates the pattern and power of Christian prayer.

Christian prayer is an imitation of the prayer of Christ, an imitation that participates in the mysteries of His life. As a child of Nazareth, Jesus made pilgrimage to the Temple; Christian prayer is also in the form of a pilgrimage to the Father's house. Because His familial piety involved a regimen of daily prayers and rituals taught by His parents from sunrise to sunset, Christians embrace the discipline of daily prayer. Because His prayer echoed in the hidden quiet of ancient Nazareth, Christian prayer must echo behind the closed doors of our bedrooms and in the heart of our homes. Because He learned to pray the psalms by

---

[10] Origen, *De Oratione*, 3.
[11] *Catechism of the Catholic Church* (hereafter CCC), 2607.

heart daily – bowing down in the morning, raising His hands like incense in the evening, and musing on His heavenly Father through the night, we must allow the affections of our own hearts to be formed by the Bible and the Liturgy of the Church.

The pattern of the prayer of Christ forms Christian prayer. After his baptism, He goes into the wilderness and devotes Himself to supplication, fasting, and resisting all forms of dehumanizing irrationality which threaten the human heart. What is begun there continues throughout His ministry. We find Him ardently in conversation with his Father through the night in deserted places, mountains and gardens. Anyone who really wants to pray also frequently withdraws for this same conversation, takes up this same struggle and strives to offer this same devotion to the Father.

Christians pray with the same confidence, power and gratitude we find in Christ. Jesus rejoices when He recognizes His Father's work. He raises His eyes to heaven. He weeps over death and prays for His friends. He is moved to tears by the plight of those who would reject Him and dies asking that even His enemies be forgiven. He blesses God and offers thanksgiving at meals, even when it appears there is not enough to eat. So powerful is His prayer that He makes the blind see, the deaf hear, the lame walk, the leprous whole, the demonically oppressed free, the dead come back to life, and the sinner forgiven. At the same time, the Lord also teaches His disciples that they will do even greater things in His Name.

By tradition, He is believed to have given His great teachings on prayer on the Mount of Olives, not far from the Garden of Gethsemane, at a place now commemorated by the Church of the *Pater Noster*. The ancient Byzantines believed Jesus ascended into heaven in the same vicinity. This hill stands between Jerusalem and Bethany, between where His enemies and His friends lived. The events recalled in this sacred geography symbolize the nature and place of all Christian prayer: listening to the Word and responding to Him, in the midst of one's friends and enemies, for their sakes, on our journey to the Father's House.

The teachings of Jesus concerning prayer are sober and straightforward. He lists petitions that ought to be prayed for, describes the interior attitudes one should adopt in prayer, and warns against using prayer to manipulate God or impress men. Although He directs his disciples to seek the Father in private solitude, He also promotes praying with others and promises to be with those who gather in His Name.

The Cross, the Eucharist and the Gift of the Spirit

By prayer He establishes a new covenant which He seals with His own Body and Blood, and this is the source and summit of all Christian prayer. His supreme wish before the Father is that His followers might dwell in unity with Him and one another in the Father. The night before He dies, He beseeches the Father with such force He sweats blood, and by so doing shows us the painful secret of love, the grace of subordinating our will to God's will. Real prayer has the form of love, and we cannot love except at our own expense.

His last wordless cry on the Cross echoes in all genuine prayer. This cry is the life breath of God flowing into the dying hearts of men and women to raise them up. At the same time, Christ's dying breath is a perfect offering to the Father of all that is humanly good and beautiful. Because its source is ever in Him, Christian prayer has the power of love, a love that cannot be conquered by death.

Now at the right hand of the Father, the eternal prayer of the Risen High Priest is forever acceptable to God. The Father is eternally pleased in the human prayer of His Divine Son. This kind of prayer is not limited by time or space because it flows from the unending source of time and space. It is no longer subject to suffering, even if it suffers for a while the rejection of an indifferent humanity. Indeed, such suffering is now subject to the Risen King, the Despoiler of Hell, the Victor over Death, and the Judge on the Last Day. Although He delays for the sake of his Mercy, the Day of Justice is ever close at hand.

The experience of the prayer of the Lord, with all its apocalyptic force, is not remote from the practicing Christian. The Holy Spirit communicates this prayer deep in the heart through a gift of grace called the Divine Indwelling. The Gift of the Holy Spirit makes the heart the dwelling place of the Holy Trinity so that the love of the Father and the Son animates the new life of the Baptized. In this way, God dwells in us to make everything that is good about our humanity sacred, a spiritual offering – from the deepest core of our innermost being to the utmost extremity of our body.

The body is animated with a transformed life to become the temple of the Holy Spirit. Through prayer, the heart is open to the indwelling love of the Father and Son so that even our most feeble sacrificial efforts to love one another in the difficult nitty-gritty circumstances of life manifest God's presence to the world. This astonishing new presence of the Trinity in the hearts of men and women causes Christians to pray with remarkable boldness even in the face of what is humanly impossible.

Besides the indwelling, there is another way the prayer of Christ is present as a living reality in the Christian life: Body and Blood, Soul and Divinity – His real presence in the Blessed Sacrament. Under the veils of bread and wine, the power of Christ's prayer issues forth into the hearts of those who partake of this mystical banquet and flows into those who behold the Eucharist with faith. By this Real Presence, He truly takes into His heart all of our deepest needs, makes them sacred in the very Blood and Water which flowed from His side, and offers them to the Father.

His Eucharistic presence, by its very nature, is never static, but always dynamic. It is the true center around which the whole Cosmos revolves and history unfolds. In perpetual thanksgiving, intercession and adoration of the Father, the dynamism of Christ's prayer by which He comes to us also draws us to Him. The loving gaze He bestows on us through the Blessed Sacrament leads us to gaze upon Him in return. This gaze of love happens in Eucharistic adoration. This can also happen whenever the call to love is generously answered.

The Loving Gaze

A beautiful witness of fixing one's gaze on this loving Presence in the 20th century occurred in Auschwitz during World War II. After an attempted escape, the commandant ordered the execution of a certain number of prisoners by starvation. One of the men chosen broke down in tears begging that he be spared for the sake of his wife and children. The commandant was shocked when a fellow prisoner volunteered to go in the man's stead. He angrily asked, "Who are you?" The man replied without hesitation, "I am a Catholic priest."

The baffled commandant accepted the substitution, and Father Maximilian Kolbe was marched with the other condemned prisoners to the starvation bunker. Deeply devoted to the Lord with a special love for the Blessed Mother, Father Kolbe helped his fellow prisoners prepare for death. He heard confessions and comforted them. They sang together and prayed.

In that dismal concentration camp, guards were attracted by the joy and peace that flowed from the bunker. The guard who finally administered Fr. Kolbe a lethal injection received pardon from the priest, the last act of the one whom Blessed John Paul II would call the *Martyr of Charity*. St. Maximilian Kolbe died with his eyes fixed on the glory of the Son of Man.

Those who discover this gaze know even in the midst of unimaginable catastrophe, He comes in power and glory. The very foundations of the world may be shaken, but rooted in Him they stand firm. Heaven and earth will pass away, but the Word made flesh will remain forever.

The Nature of Christian Prayer

The prayers of those who believe in the Lord are infused with this eschatological urgency, this apocalyptic awareness. This is because Christian prayer is about listening with one's whole being. Such listening welcomes the Word made flesh into the inner sanctuary of the heart. In this intimacy, the Christ communicates the fullness of life to the soul and the soul is animated with His thoughts and desires. The desires and thoughts of the Heart of Christ in which they share are all oriented to the glory of the Father and the completion of His work in the world.

Those who embrace this risen humanity, who take on the likeness of this Heavenly Man, begin to bind themselves to His perpetual state of supernatural activity: it can be an ecstasy and crucifixion all at once. These Christians are not so mindful of what they are undergoing as much as they are fixated on the wonders the Lord is accomplishing. Before His Holy Face, they weep over the plight of the downtrodden, scrutinize their own lack of love, and see only the immensity of His mercy.

Cleaving to Christ in faith renders one vulnerable to wonder filled adoration before the excessiveness of Triune love. This kind of prayer searches out divine glory. It discovers this glory forever unfolding in an eternal moment, captivating every thought. Ancient splendors of God shine in unpredictably new ways in the substance of those who hold fast, even when they are completely unaware that anything of importance is happening. Their hearts know fear of the Lord, holy sorrow and uncontained jubilation all at once. This is a baptism in love, the love that lives in the heart of the One who is coming to judge the living and the dead.

27

The Heart of Christ bears the great tension between God's mercy and human misery. Because humanity connects us together, when He went deep into prayer, He found our wounds, embraced them and offered them to the Father. The depths to which He did this are disclosed on the Cross.

When we behold the wounds which He received from us, we discover the wounds we have inflicted on ourselves and each other. Through taking our brokenness and making it His own by love, He has completely implicated Himself in our misery, completely identified Himself with our plight so that we never suffer alone.

Because of what the Lord has done for us, we always have reason to hope. As the integrity of our old humanity succumbs to the futility to which it is subject, by faith a new sacred humanity is already born: more powerful than death, capable of filling each moment with a fullness of love, and by each act of love, no matter how hidden, revealing in a unique and un-repeatable manner the glory of God, man fully alive.

The prayer of this new humanity is the school in which Christ teaches us to trust God. He constantly comes into our hearts in remarkable and astonishing ways. He approaches us searching, knocking, thirsting, begging, waiting for that moment of mutual recognition where at last we will realize how loved we really are.

He also whispers anew the subtle wisdom of God in the face of our foolishness. With great hope in us, He invites us to bear with Him His concern for the plight of humanity, especially the poor, both those materially and spiritually indigent. Will His questioning glance pierce us to the heart?

Conversatio morum — one's whole manner of life constantly submitted to Christ

His mysterious question allows us to question ourselves, to take account of where we are in our lives. When we hear this question in our hearts and try to answer it, we engage in what St. Benedict and other saints spoke of as *conversatio morum.* This is an ongoing commitment to examine every aspect of one's life in light of the Gospel and to submit everything to Christ every moment of each day come what come may.

Conversion of life begins by conversation with God about everything. He initiates the dialogue of salvation but we must be active participants. This means silencing our other activities to attend to his voice.

Prayer requires regular periods of silent listening to the Word made flesh. This requires that we be open and vulnerable not only to what He has said but also to his very person present by faith. One is only really listening when one welcomes the other into his heart.

We must discern what the Risen Lord makes known to us about our lives and motives. He admonishes those He loves and encourages those of whom He has great expectations. If we are attentive, His voice becomes the beacon by which we find our way out of a jungle of guilt and into the friendship for which we were made.

Conversatio morum is not a one-time event, but an ongoing re-examination of our lives in light of the Gospel of Christ. It is a journey, a pilgrimage of faith. Repentance and continual conversion mark the way. The English verb "to repent" comes from the Latin *re-pentare,* to re-think or to think in a new way.

The more we go down the pathway of faith, the more we learn to think like Christ. Certain things we deem of little importance when we first set out take on a specific gravity the more we think like the Lord. We come to see that little habits that we did not think were so bad are actually of great concern to God.

For example, irreverent humor about the things of the Lord might be taken lightly in the beginning. After enduring difficult trials and great suffering, a soul can be filled with tender gratitude that is repulsed by even a slight suggestion of irreverence. This new sensitivity is what tradition knows as fear of the Lord and it is the beginning of wisdom.

Repentance leads to conversion, the turning of our lives away from lesser things and back to God. When we begin to think about ourselves and the world the way Christ sees them and allow this new thinking to change the way we live, we not only apply the brakes to a certain momentum in our lives, but we also change our overall direction. Christ sees the world with resurrected eyes – eyes not blinded by the fear of death. His vision gives us a certain audacity in dealing with our own shortcomings and in trying to do something beautiful for God. Instead of going away from God, when we see what Christ sees, we begin to draw close to Him.

The Primacy of Grace

For this to happen however there is a fundamental principle that needs to be stressed today more than ever. This principle is the primacy of grace. Stressing this principle today is important because we live in a time of "self-help" books. Such works can be informative and even helpful. Often, however, many authors offer little more than fantastic hubris when it comes to the spiritual life. No human wisdom can replace what only a living relationship with the Risen Lord provides.

Christ renews our minds and changes our thinking by sanctifying grace – a gift by which we participate in the very life of God. Grace causes a living encounter with the Lord. It is a pure and undeserved gift that flows from the heart of Him who was pierced for our offenses and is risen from the dead. Divinely endowed, this new life permeates and raises the very substance of our soul, making the inner essence of our humanity holy in the sight of God.

Even when the spiritual life involves difficult renunciation or persevering through an impossible trial, the reason such heroism is possible is because of the grace of Christ. Every Christian knows that when he is really tested, it is only God's grace that sees him through. His power is made perfect in our weakness, and in the end all glory and honor belong to Him alone.

This means that we need to ask the Lord for what we do not have if we are to make a good beginning in the life of prayer. Christian prayer bears a petitionary character for this reason. Grace is given to those who ask.

Consider the father who went to Jesus for his son's sake in the Gospel of Mark. His son was afflicted with a deadly spirit which caused irrational and dangerous behavior. He wanted Jesus' help, but because his son's misery seemed so insurmountable, he was not unconditionally confident in his petition. What parent can fail to identify with this paternal anxiety?

Jesus was able to answer this anxiety because He fully understands every heart that comes to him. He hears our most secret sorrows and feels our emptiness because He has entered into the same mud from which we are made. In the face of the father's plight, He did the most loving thing he could do. Jesus discretely admonished the distressed father for his disbelief. The doubt that up to that moment had plagued the father's heart was laid bare.

Until his doubt was recognized, the man was not free to have faith, the kind of faith he needed for his son's sake. His own dignity as the father of his son was impaired by his self-ignorance. Jesus' word, however, helped the man see the truth. We are ever vulnerable to irrational malice because of our lack of trust in God.

This gentle rebuke stirred the man to the kind of faith he needed. The word of Christ helped him humbly recognize the lack of faith from which he suffered, and with this recognition, to find the courage to submit his doubt to the Lord. A confident and truthful prayer emerged from the depths of his heart, "Lord, I believe, help my disbelief" Mark 9:24.

Prayer as a Moment of Truth

Christian prayer because it is a graced filled encounter with Christ anticipates going before the judgment seat of God. This is something each of us must do at the moment of death. We can either spend our lives trying to avoid this moment or we can prepare for it. Prayer prepares us to welcome the judgment of the Lord.

When we turn to prayer, we are making a decision to submit ourselves to the judgment of the Lord. He does not condemn, but He is concerned about honesty and accountability. It is a matter of vulnerability and truth before God. As painful as this is, it is a mere preparation for something much more. Accepting the judgment of the Lord opens us to deep movements of the heart in which we see how vulnerable God has made Himself to us.

Since the Lord loves us, why are we afraid of the judgment of the Lord? Perhaps it is because we know that there is something in us that is hostile to the loving presence of God and the demands of love. To really understand the way prayer anticipates our final judgment, this distaste for prayer needs to be scrutinized further.

Have you ever noticed after being invited to visit a nursing home, or to pray the Stations of the Cross, or to do some other good work that, instead of being grateful for the opportunity, there is a certain aversion, even a peculiar dread that takes hold? Even if we suffer this feeling only momentarily, this is a glimpse into a kind of hostility we bear to God. If this propensity to sin is never addressed, it inclines us to an alienating misery. Most Christians are scarcely aware of just how much this robs them of the joy of knowing the Lord and of living by His love.

We resist many gentle promptings to pray because of this tendency to see our Creator in opposition to us. What we think we want for ourselves seems in conflict with what the Lord asks

32

of us. Religion, piety, holiness feel burdensome, an inconvenience, an imposition on our lives. We want our liberty, and the Lord, with His moral standards, seems to want to take it away. We want to be in control of our own destiny, and the Author of our freedom insists that we submit our lives to Him instead. Our freewill and His divine will seem mutually exclusive.

We do not want to submit this hostility to the scrutiny of the Lord in prayer because we are afraid of what we might lose or what might happen. We resist prayer, because we are resistant to the truth. Biblically, this is called hardness of heart.

If prayer is a trial for our hardened hearts, another fear, reverent fear of the Lord, helps us suffer this crisis with humility. This is not a servile fear of punishment; it is the holy fear that love knows. It is a gift that the Lord gives so that we might find the courage to approach Him rightly.

The relationship of holy fear and openness to the truth is rooted in love. Love does not resist the truth. True love eagerly awaits it. Reverence establishes love in the truth.

In true humble prayer we permit God to question the hostility that weighs us down. The Lord's questioning puts before us the truth about who He is and the truth who we are before Him. Only in this truth, the truth of divine judgment, do we have the opportunity to be lifted up in radical freedom before His goodness.

What is radical freedom? Though wounded by sin, our natural freedom is a gift from the Lord. This gift of liberty gives us the potential to live by love. But to realize this, our freedom needs to be purified from the evil which diminishes it.

God respects our freedom too much to impose His goodness on us. He waits until we ask, and we do not ask until we have nothing to lose. It is when we recognize how desperate our plight actually is that we discover the freedom to act on his interior promptings to turn to Him.

We live fully when we enter freely into the mystery of the Lord's love. Existence outside of this love is vulnerable to all kinds of unnecessary difficulties. In His great love, He protects us from most of these evils. He does not want us to lose hope even when we reject Him or put Him off. Only when it is necessary will He make use of a difficult situation to fulfill His plan of love.

In accord with His plan of love, the Lord may mysteriously permit us to come against a devastating hardship. It is important to note that He permits but He does not cause the hardship. God does not will evil. He is never vindictive. At the same time, He loves us too much to allow us to live in dangerous falsehoods.

The Lord wants us to face the actual situation we are in. Falsehoods prevent us from doing this. For example, it is common to be under the illusion that we are pretty good people, that while others may be wicked, we are ourselves "okay" overall. We think we can put off going to confession, or doing penance, or prayer, because "it is not that bad." If we think this, then we will never know how much we need Christ to save us. We will never get the help we need.

Here, to free us from this illusion of self-sufficiency, an external difficulty may sometimes be permitted to put us in touch with the truth about our interior plight. Sometimes our situation is so precarious; permitting us to undergo such a trial is the only way He has left to dispose us to turn to Him.

The divine impact: this is what Elisabeth of the Trinity calls it. God's fullness and human emptiness: the collision of these opposing forces is dangerous. The Lord does not want this moment to destroy us, but He also yearns for our friendship, and friendship with Him requires this dangerous encounter. He suffered this moment in his own humanity to show us the way and now through prayer He enters into our lives that we might bear this divine impact in our own hearts. Unless we embrace this moment with Him, our hostility thwarts the desire of His Heart.

This is why He chose to die for us: so that we might know this moment. By allowing the violence of our hearts to spend itself against His ardent desire for our love, He found the pathway by which He could descend into the depths of our misery so that we would not have to suffer this alone, without Him. He is with us in our hardships, especially those that drive us to reach out to Him.

The Word became flesh to gain access into the painful places of our lives. He had to make Himself vulnerable, capable of being pierced by us, if He was to find a way of piercing our hard hearts without completely destroying us. In doing so, He shows us the pattern of Christian prayer.

The Pattern of Christian Prayer

Our misery has drawn God's mercy, and His mercy has taken the form of the Cross. Christ's descent into hell speaks to this. If pious tradition suggests He went in search of our first parents on Holy Saturday, this is in harmony with the fact that He searches for each of us in the weaknesses, secret sorrows and other wounds that mark so much of our mortal existence.[12] He has won the right to endure these hardships for us by the power of the Cross. Through the Cross He has turned even our rejection of God into an occasion of grace. Through the Cross, He has gained access to every heart.

When we are finally humbled in our suffering, we realize that we do not know how to pray. But if we look to Jesus, we see that He has suffered with us and in a mysterious way He is praying for us in our suffering just as He prayed in His own suffering.

---

[12] Compare the ancient homily read for the *Office of Readings* on Holy Saturday with 1 Peter 3:18-20 and Ephesians 4:8-9.

Because He became fully man, He gave us an example of how to sanctify the dirt and grit of life by prayer. Because He is eternally God, He was able to sow a new experience of divine power in the depths of this mud. He continues to do this today at the right hand of the Father; and, for this reason, the dynamism of Christ's prayer is both a historical reality and an ever unfolding mystical power until the end of time.

Christ's prayer in history continues now in mystery. Our liturgy is rooted in this. His eternal relationship with the Father never changes even as He transforms all of creation. Christian prayer is, therefore, essentially a relational reality, a personal encounter between God and man, made possible by Christ.

The Testimonies at the End of the 2ⁿᵈ Millennium

The primacy of grace in prayer has the form of a loving invitation. A young Polish girl was at a dance. She was trying, unsuccessfully, to have a good time. In her heart, she wanted to do something beautiful for God. A couple years before, she asked her parents if she could enter a convent. They refused her request. Instead, she was working as a housekeeper, trying to fit in with everybody else. It was not working.

As she started to dance, she saw Jesus. Stripped and scourged, the Lord gazed into the eyes of the young lady and asked, "How long will you keep putting me off?"[13]

Helen Kowalska quietly left the dance and ran to a church to listen to the Lord. She felt the Lord call her to go to Warsaw to enter a convent. Like Abraham, she obeyed immediately, going home to settle her affairs and explain to her sister what had happened. Trusting in Divine Providence, she went without knowing exactly which convent she was to enter. Instead, she chose to

---

[13] Saint Maria Faustina Kowalska, *Diary: Divine Mercy in My Soul*, Stockbridge, MA: Marian Press (2008) 7.

make herself generously available to whatever the Lord had in store for her.

This began a great pattern in her life and prayer. Christ would ask her to do things; as she learned to obey Him, their conversation together deepened. Through prayer, she learned to trust Jesus, to live her life rooted in Him.

She would only live for another thirteen years, largely misunderstood and thought to be delusional by most those with whom she lived in community. Mysteriously, ridicule and rejection opened her heart to the Lord in even deeper ways. She discovered in her encounters with the Lord not only the joy and freedom of knowing Him, but also a truth the whole world needed to know: the message of divine mercy. The message she promoted, until her death in 1938, would come to sustain many Catholics during and after the apocalyptic events of World War II. Canonized by Pope John Paul II, Saint Faustina Kowalska has become among the most influential saints of the 20th Century.

A note on the remarkable vision of Jesus that started St. Faustina on her pilgrimage of faith: To see Jesus, to behold him with our hearts, can take place in the form of an actual vision we see or an impression left on the eyes of our soul. Sometimes in the writings of the great saints and mystics, it seems they either do not care about such distinctions or else they are not aware of them.

Once someone has encountered the Lord, in whatever way He has been felt or experienced, how it happened exactly becomes subordinate to what exactly happened. It can happen when we are deep in silence. It can also happen when we are not expecting it. This is because there is no limit to the ways God can choose to disclose Himself. In Christian prayer, God's action comes before human action.

Before moving on to our next chapter, I would like to touch briefly on something St. Faustina believed Jesus told her about His loving presence. It illustrates that the presence of the

Lord is very personal and that Jesus takes our attitudes seriously. This means He finds the less than generous spiritual games we play to be painful:

> I wait for souls, and they are indifferent toward Me. I love them tenderly and sincerely, and they distrust Me. I want to lavish My graces on them and they do not want to accept them. They treat me as a dead object.[14]

On one level, the glorified humanity of Christ Risen from the dead is no longer subject to the misery of this world. However, from the standpoint of His great love for us, the desire He has for union with us, Christ who constantly intercedes on our behalf can be pained by our lack of faith and gratitude. Christian prayer does not reach out to some impersonal force. Instead, it is interpersonal, an *I – thou* relationship, a heart to heart. We must humbly bear in mind that the Lord has real expectations in our conversations with Him.

To illuminate this further, it will be helpful to refer to one more great light for our times. St. Therese of Lisieux, Doctor of the Church, died several years before Sr. Faustina was born. Their messages converge on the mercy of the Lord. St. Therese not only deeply understood this passion in the Lord's heart, she felt it and it moved her:

> He thirsts for love. Ah, I feel it more than ever – Jesus is suffering thirst. He only meets ingratitude and indifference over and over among the disciples of the world. Among his own disciples he finds (*This is so overwhelming!*)

---

[14] Dairy #1447 as cited in Saint Maria Faustina Kowalska, *Diary: Divine Mercy in My Soul*, Stockbridge, MA: Marian Press (2008) 511.

so few hearts surrendering themselves to him without reserve, understanding the tenderness of his love.[15]

His heart yearns for us to come to Him without reserve, with complete trust. We can be indifferent only as long as we refuse His loving gaze. To search for and accept this this gaze of the Lord seems to be the key to the teachings of both St. Faustina and St. Therese. Indeed, the thirst of Jesus in the face of our indifference is a great theme of the 20th Century. Mother Theresa of Calcutta understood this and in all her chapels, next to the crucifix and over the altar one sees the words, "I thirst."

---

[15] LT 196, Therese wrote to Sr. Marie of the Sacred Heart right around Sept. 13, 1896, trying to provide her with an explanation for her approach to the spiritual life. Translation my own.

Chapter Two

Where Doubt and Faith Collide

Doubt is the starting place for many who are seeking a deeper relationship with the Lord. This can come in many forms, yet we can articulate it in the form of a question: Is what I believe really real? The only answer to such a question is prayer. Prayer does not shield us from doubt. It baptizes our hearts in all kinds of doubts and difficulties, trials and tests. Violently opposing forces, faith confronts doubt in prayer.

Doubt is an inescapable part of life. Christians are not the only ones who must deal with doubt. In our introduction, we mentioned the story of Anthony Bloom. This story is really about the doubt of an atheist. Even someone who does not believe in God still has doubts to face. For example, what if one's belief that God does not exist is false and what if what the Christians claim is true after all? [16] Prayer, for this atheist, became the compelling answer to this existential question.

For many saints and mystics, doubt became an affliction entrusted to them by Christ. It seems strange to write this. It must be even stranger to read it. Why would Christ entrust those He loves with an affliction, especially an affliction like doubt? The answer is to be found in the way Christ chose to save us.

Jesus did not brush over our human experience but fully entered into it – enjoying and suffering to the last drop everything about our life in this world, except sin itself. Although He never acted in disobedience to His Father in Heaven, Christ shared with us the consequences of our disobedience, humbly embracing even

---

[16] This insight is discussed by Joseph Ratzinger, now Pope Benedict XVI, in *Introduction to Christianity*, trans. J.R. Foster, San Francisco: Communio Books, Ignatius Press (1990) 15-21.

death itself. Although He never doubted, He did share with us the sometimes dehumanizing anguish that doubt can engender in those who love or want to love God. Consider the recourse Jesus makes to Psalm 22 during his passion. Although it ultimately becomes a prayer of confidence in God, the psalm begins with a crucified man's agonizing question to God, "Why have you abandoned me?"

By saving us in this way, even to the point of bearing the suffering our doubts cause us, Jesus opens all of human experience to the mercy of God. Mercy is love which suffers the misery of another in such a way that the person's dignity is affirmed. Jesus, by sharing the suffering that our doubts cause us, transforms this anguish into a kind of spiritual place where we can discover His presence.

This is an important principle for the spiritual life. God does not make our sufferings magically go away. He transforms them and endows them with new meaning so that rather than diminish our humanity, suffering becomes a pathway to friendship with Him. Suffering, trials, difficulties with the faith, these are all places of a genuine encounter with God in love. It is in these places where human limitations and divine limitlessness embrace. In this embrace, in this encounter, we know the actualization of all it means to be fully human and fully alive.

The Witness of St. Therese of Lisieux

This helps us to understand the great spiritual trials of saints like Therese of Lisieux to whom we referred at the end of our last chapter.[17] A Carmelite nun she lived a life of intense prayer and friendship with the Lord. In the last months of her life, after suffering for more than two years from tuberculosis, she was ordered to finish her autobiography. She begins by explain-

---

[17] Pope Benedict also refers to this Doctor of the Church in his discussion cited above.

ing the great joy and peace the Lord had blessed her with in Carmel but then goes on to describe a trial she is facing.

It is important to note that in the Christian life of prayer,
spiritual maturity does not consist in an absence of suffering. Maturity in the faith is instead the ability to suffer with a deep spiritual joy and an invincible peace which nothing in this world can
take away. This joy is the joy of possessing Jesus even when He
feels absence. This peace is the peace the Lord gives us even as
the storms of life surge around us.

If we persevere in prayer and allow Christ to raise us to
full spiritual maturity, this joy and peace do not diminish suffering. In fact, with this fruit of the Spirit, the Christian is able to suffer even more to a great heroic degree. He is given what he needs
to pick up his cross. Those who follow Christ Crucified live a life
of increasing vulnerability to all kinds of trials and difficulties.
This is where love leads. Yet these are always crosses they can
bear because the strength of the Lord bears it in them.

Any person of prayer knows that in intense suffering,
there is a special presence of Christ which, even when it feels as
though He is absent, provides an inner strength and a spiritual
fruitfulness. This is not always felt at the time. It is often something that is realized only afterward. This kind of presence of the
Lord is not a matter of feeling or thinking. It is deeper than the
operation of our psychological faculties.

So when St. Therese says she has joy and peace, she is not
merely saying what a religious person ought to say. She is articu-
lating an insight that she discovered in her suffering. Yet, what
she goes on to say about this joy and peace helps us see that
Christ's special presence in her suffering does not shield her from
very painful experiences. She recounts only weeks before her
death:

> Jesus made me feel that there were really souls who have
> no faith, and who, through the abuse of grace, lost this

precious treasure, the source of the only real and pure joys. He permitted my soul to be invaded by the thickest darkness, and that the thought of heaven, up until then so sweet to me, became no longer anything but the cause of struggle and torment. This trial was to last not a few days or a few weeks, it was not to be extinguished until the hour set by God Himself and this hour has not yet come.[18]

The reason why this darkness was a particular trial was that in the past, when suffering difficult times, she was able to sustain herself by entering into deep prayer and resting in the thought of heaven. Now, the thought of heaven was almost impossible to bear. It was not that she did not believe such a place existed. She just could not believe that she would be able to go there and be happy. Whatever light heaven offered, she felt, was not being offered to her when it would seem most useful. Just what beatitude really was, as opposed to what she imagined it to be, seems to have deeply troubled her spirit.

We are considering Therese's experience to explain why God not only allows those He loves to suffer the effects of doubt, but also even entrusts them with the very darkness that those without faith suffer. God is absent to those without faith and sometimes He feels absent to those who do believe in Him. Sometimes God feels absent because we have abandoned Him by not living by faith. This is called backsliding. There are also times He feels absent even when we have been faithful.

When God withdraws His presence from the feelings or thoughts of a faithful believer, there may be many mysterious reasons for this. One thing is certain: the follower of Christ is being given in this experience of God's absence an opportunity to enter into the plight of those who do not know God. The Christian in these circumstances is sharing in the plight of others who need the

---

[18] *Story of a Soul: the Autobiography of St. Therese of Lisieux*, trans. John Clarke, O.C.D., Washington, D.C.:ICS (1975, 1976, 3rd ed. 1996) 211-212.

Lord. To learn to love and to pray in these conditions requires that we live by faith.

To live by faith means to be faithful to Him even when our feelings, our thoughts, our imagination cannot find Him. This is a trial of faith, a small simple way to express our gratitude to the Lord for all He has done for us. Such trials root us even deeper in the Lord and his saving mercy.

This trial of spiritual darkness can be so overbearing we can feel tempted to doubt, to forsake our life of faith. Yet suffering the darkness that causes people to doubt is not the same as doubting. The darkness is an ordeal but not a sin. Doubt, on the other hand, is a choice. When in the face of difficult darkness we renounce doubt and choose to believe in God's love, our faith becomes radically strong.

Christians can suffer the darkness of doubt even if they do not doubt but believe. The extent to which Christ has already suffered the darkness invading every heart is revealed on the Cross. He has descended into our darkest experiences so that we would not suffer alone, so that in looking at Him, we might recover our dignity.

If someone is struggling with such darkness in his own life, it is still possible to believe even in the face of such overbearing difficulty. When we choose to believe in spite of such darkness, when we raise our hearts in prayer even when it feels like there is no reason to do so, this is when we are in special solidarity with the Lord. In solidarity with Him, we free Him to do great things through us.

Saint Therese, in fact, before she received this trial, had asked Jesus to use her in a special way to extend his mercy to those who most needed it. To answer such a beautiful petition, to allow her to help extend the mercy of God to those who most needed it, the Lord would need to allow Therese to share in the darkness that afflicted those furthest from Him. Under the crushing logic of doubt, they did not feel hope but only the banal weight of meaninglessness. In solidarity with them, Therese confronted in her own heart this overwhelming effect of doubt even as she battled to believe.

As she faced her own terminal illness, she entered into the battle of faith, the contest against doubt that is won only through prayer. Struggling to believe in the love of God, she learned on a much deeper level to beg for mercy for herself and for those whose misery she shared. Her prayer entered into the depths of a deeper love, a more encompassing compassion. God allowed her to suffer such an intense struggle with doubt because of the immeasurable good that prayer can do when the love with which we pray is purified and deepened. Only through suffering all kinds of trials and hardships is the love with which we pray made perfect.

This is the thing about suffering anything for God's sake – the greater the love by which our sacrifices are offered, the greater the space in our hearts for God's power to be unleashed in the world. Spiritual space in the heart is the capacity to give God the freedom to move in us and act in us with His saving love. Giving God this freedom requires that we die to ourselves sometimes in regards to very good things.

St. Therese was moved to surrender even the joy that the thought of heaven once gave her so that God's love could teach her compassion for those who did not believe in anything beyond this life. In doing this, she gave God space, the freedom to give something even greater than the fleeting (a) joy the thought of heaven can give. Her suffering allowed the joy of heaven to enter the world in better ways.

To accept such a cross is to participate in Christ's work of redemption. Such participation is possible because the mystery of the Cross is superabundant with vast space for our own works of love to extend its power in cooperation with Him. Because prayer opens the heart to this freedom of Christ, it is decisive for confronting doubt with faith.

The experience of St. Therese of Lisieux invites us to consider how those who join themselves to Christ by faith are invited by Him to share in this saving mission, to bear the misery that afflicts those who have, to varying degrees, rejected God. If we begin prayer feeling like we are afflicted with painful doubts and difficulties, we must ask how we have abused the graces richly bestowed on us. We must also ask what it is that Christ is entrusting to us now, what it is that He is asking us to bear with Him.

It is in the experience of doubt that both atheists and Christians are bound to each other in some way. The human condition is filled with so many riddles very few of which can be solved. This is why we are forbidden to judge one another, and more than this, it is the reason we must learn to bear with one another. We do not ever fully know the questions that anyone suffers in his heart, and we cannot know exactly how the Lord will answer. All we know is that even in the face of doubts and painful questions the answer is found in seeking the Lord with humble courage.

Doubt and all kinds of difficulties with our faith come in many shades and hues. There is the feeling that God is not there or that some proposition of the faith either is not true in general, or at least, is not true for me. Then there is the more subtle variety. The kind of which we are scarcely aware, which drives our lives in ways we do not fully understand. This is a practical atheism.

Those living with this un-chosen belief might be able to talk about the Lord in convincing terms. They may have good morals and religious practices. Yet all their religion is on the outside. They are not engaged in any real *conversatio morum* because, in the practical day-to-day way they get by in life, they go on as if the Lord were not a living personal reality in their lives.

The Witness of St. Teresa of Avila

The spiritual conversion of Teresa de Ahumada speaks to how Christ's love gives the humble the courage we need in begin-

46

ning to pray. Teresa was born in 1515, and her mother died when she was only thirteen. At the age of twenty, against her father's will, she snuck off to become a Carmelite nun.

She enjoyed religious life and was good at it. Everyone thought that because she looked so pious, she was holy. She, however, came to feel vexed about her lack of devotion to the Lord.

After almost twenty years of religious life, she felt her external practices to be little more than an empty show. In her heart, she was holding back from the Lord, afraid to trust Him, afraid to really pray. She was unhappy with herself, but unable to do anything about it.

An unexpected grace changed all this. On her way to liturgy with her community, Teresa of Avila glanced at a statue of Christ which depicted Him after the scourging. Her eyes met His and she experienced the Lord looking at her with love. This loving presence of the Lord was so intense, the Mother of the Carmelite Reform in Spain and future Doctor of the Church, knelt down in tears, begging the Lord, determined not to stop praying until He gave her the grace to make a new beginning.[19]

True humility attracts God. Humility regulates how we esteem ourselves. The word humility itself derives from the Latin *humus* which means rich fertile soil. This suggests the great primordial truth of our origins.

Man was fashioned from the dust of the earth, and at the end of his days, he returns to it. God breathed his life into mud and made it capable of doing something divine. Life is a very fragile gift lavished upon us when we have done nothing to deserve it. We have only a very brief time to make of it something beautiful for God. God is attracted to souls that ground their

---

[19] She relates this story herself in *The Book of her Life*, Chapter 9, in *The Collected Works of St. Teresa of Avila*, vol. 1, trans. Kieran Kavanaugh O.C.D. and Otilio Rodriguez O.C.D., Washington, D.C.: ICS (2002), 100-104.

lives in this truth. Such humility permits Him to accomplish great things.

A particular kind of courage needs to go with such humility: the courage to accept ourselves, including our weaknesses. Romano Guardini distinguishes this sort of courage from bravery.[20] Bravery confronts things that threaten us from without. Courage, from this perspective, helps us confront what is within us. This is not the same as excusing our own sinfulness. It is a matter of humbly accepting the truth about ourselves, courageously acknowledging we need God's help.

Spiritual Misery and the Wounds of Sin

Why really do we doubt God? We began to develop this theme when we considered prayer as a moment of judgment in the last chapter. Here, we look at the hostility that inflicts us as an absence of love. Humility, the disposition whereby we esteem ourselves the way God esteems us, accepts the reality of sin but never loses hope in God.

Where love is absent, there is every form of misery. Such privations of love in the recesses of the heart are the wounds of sin: sins we have committed and sins committed by others against us – even the sin of our first parents, Original Sin. These wounds rob us of our confidence in the Lord. Only when we allow the inexhaustible mercy of God to confront this misery are the doubts that haunt us about God addressed.

So many good people who want to serve God complain that they do not pray because they do not have time. But might it be that the reason they do not have time for prayer is that they have not made prayer the priority of their heart? If we were to go further and look at the reason prayer is not our priority, we discover disbelief, doubt. It is hard to be committed to something if

---

[20] See *Learning the Virtues that Lead to God*, trans. Stella Lange with revisions, Manchester, NH: Sophia Institute Press (1998), 197ff.

whether it is really real is in question. Haunting us is that question with which we started this reflection: What if it is not really real?

Anyone who feels this way almost always thinks that such doubts are not really dealt with in Christianity. Teresa of Avila experienced how tempting it is to simply pretend and muddle through doubts and questions because (we assume) this is how everyone else is doing it. She went to Church; she learned the ritual of religious life; she knew how to impress everyone with her piety.

She even pretended to pray, and in pretending instead of really trying, she soon discovered that she was losing her ability to do so altogether. Anyone who knows this experience should realize that he has ventured into one of the most disconcerting doctrines of our faith. To live like this is to discover that rejecting Christ is a real possibility that lives in false piety.

To help us understand this possibility, the Gospels narrate the story of the rich young man and his encounter with Christ. He brought to Christ his deepest life question, "What must I do?" In the face of the Lord's answer, he lost heart and went away sad. As long as our gaze does not meet His, as long as we do not search for the Lord in prayer, Christ's answer to our doubt is very difficult to accept. This is because the Lord asks from us what He asked from the young man: humble obedience.

The Humble Obedience of Prayer

Teresa of Avila well understood even before her conversion that prayer demands obedience to the Lord. She feared what the Lord would ask and she feared not being able to be faithful to it. Prayer went against her instinct for self-preservation.

Obedience requires us to act against our instinct for self-preservation. Can we really thrive if we act against this instinct? Against this instinct, encountering Christ in prayer passes through the Cross. The Cross is a mystery that requires the surrender of our reputation, security, comfort, and control. Can we actually surrender these things to God?

How does one pray in the face of this kind of doubt? Tormenting ourselves over what we might lose is a dead end. We need to keep our eyes fixed on what lies ahead. The obedience of prayer does not primarily concern what we do or what we give up. Obedience is primarily a matter of listening and welcoming the Word of the Father into our hearts. This kind of prayer receives the Lord and allows Him freedom to disclose Himself.

St. Teresa shows us that prayer begins when we discover Jesus looking at us with love. Accepting His love overcomes our doubts. This obedient prayer responds with a humble, simple decision. The response is a movement of the heart to cling to Jesus no matter what. In her case, she resolved not to get off her knees until the Lord granted her the grace to pray and not fall away from prayer again.

The difficulties surrounding faith never magically go away. Yet because she would not move until the Lord helped her, she was given something to deal with all the difficulties that plagued her. This determination to rely on the Lord is one of the dimensions to true obedience.

No nice neat formula or technique or program assuaged her disbelief. Instead, discovering the gaze of Christ's love even in the midst of her inner vexation occasioned the beginning of the most beautiful and intense prayer. Her example gives us reason to take heart even if beginning to pray seems pointless.

Prayer and Authenticity

In authentic Christian prayer, every ideological head must bow, every cause driven knee must bend and every social agenda spun tongue must declare that Jesus Christ is Lord. Similarly, techniques, methods and forms of piety are secondary to being in right relationship with the Lord. This does not mean that various kinds of vocal prayer or ways of meditation are not helpful. It is just that reading the Bible, praying the Rosary, or entering into silence are all subordinate to being reconciled with God and cleaving to Him by faith.

The authenticity of Christian devotion comes from Christ. He reconciles us to God. The eyes of faith see His arms wide outstretched. Confidence springs from our belief in His cruciform love, a love that is stronger than death, more powerful than even our indifference and aversion to Him. It is when our gaze meets His that we feel a cry resound in our heart, the cry that resounds in every true disciple's heart, *"Lord, teach us how to pray!"*

When the Lord taught his disciples to pray, the only technique He promoted was humble petition and simple thanksgiving. The humble simplicity of the Lord's Prayer speaks to the most beautiful movements of heart that one can know before the face of God. The Lord wanted disciples to pray with unshakeable confidence and vulnerability before our Heavenly Father. To this end, He also used signs, bread and wine in particular. These signs help us abandon ourselves to the Father just as He did.

This introduces us to the wisdom by which Christian prayer begins with the Sign of the Cross. [21] The Catholic faith has always based itself in concrete, tangible, and sacred signs. Something about the incarnation of the Word in the womb of Mary and the resurrection of Christ in the flesh has made visible things capable of communicating spiritual reality. Our sacred patrimony insists on an incarnate tradition of prayer in which bodily posture and gestures are important.

---

[21] *Catechism of the Catholic Church*, #2157.

Chapter Three
De signaculo sanctae crucis

Since ancient times, Christians have begun to pray by blessing themselves with the Sign of the Cross. No one really knows how old this sign actually is. By 204 A.D., Tertullian, a father of the western the theological tradition, is already referring to *"signaculo sanctae crucis"* as ancient practice.[22] This blessing roots our prayer in our redemption, our baptism, our faith, our Church and our Lord himself.[23]

The Church entrusts this sign to catechumens as they prepare to enter the waters of baptism. It is a physical, bodily expression of prayer rooted in the bloody work of redemption Christ offered with his own body. Just as Christ's physical death establishes our communion in Him, we share that communion with one another through our bodies, through even the sacred gestures we make to call to mind what He has done.

It is through the body that we disclose the truth about ourselves to one another. Christian prayer is not a disembodied endeavor: it has a physical dimension to it because the Christian faith is an embodied faith – a faith in spiritual truth that must be expressed in our very flesh and blood.

Once he enters the waters of baptism, the Christian's body is made a member of the Lord's body. His very life is no longer his own and his body is no longer to be used for sin. Instead, alt-

---

[22] In defending a Christian soldier persecuted for refusing to wear the military garland, Tertullian discusses these traditional Christian practices. See *De Corona Militis*.

[23] Jean Danielou discusses its origins as related to baptism in *The Bible and the Liturgy*, University of Notre Dame Press; Notre Dame, Indiana (April 2002).

hough he will often fall short, everything he does in life is to be an offering of love for the glory of God.

This means a radical and ongoing changing of one's ways, a total re-examination of every aspects of one's life in the face of God's love – the *conversatio morum* to which great ascetics dedicated themselves throughout the history of the Church. The Sign of the Cross is the beginning of a conversation with the Lord about the whole manner of one's life. In this holy conversation, Christ crucified helps us see how every thought, every decision, every moment can become something beautiful for God.

In this spirit, Tertullian describes this sign as a regular part of Christian life at every step along the way, whether coming or going. In his view, it is a sign that sanctifies the most ordinary of activities: putting on shoes, taking a bath, sharing meals, and even lighting a candle. Applied to our own day, there is nothing wrong with making this sign in our cars at the beginning or ending of a trip, in an airliner at take-off or landing, or else getting on or off any form of public transportation. It is pious practice to make the sign to thank God for good news or to ask for help when we find ourselves in the face of danger. Whether we are on the way home or headed out for the day, relaxing in our chairs or going to work, getting up in the morning or going to bed; no matter what, he says, "we make the Sign of the Cross."[24]

The visible gesture signifies an invisible reality, the spiritual relationship between the Christian and the Risen Lord.[25] In the West, this is done by extending the fingers of one's open right hand to touch first the forehead, then just below the chest, then from the left shoulder to the right before folding one's hands in prayer. This action is accompanied by an invocation of the Trinity

---

[24] My own paraphrased translation of *De Corona Militis*, 3 *Ad omnem progressum atque promotum, ad omnem ditum et exitum, ad uestitum, ad calciatum, ad lauacra, ad mensas, ad lumina, ad cubilia, ad sedilia,qua cumque nos conuersatio exercet, frontem signaculo terimus.*
[25] See *Catechism of the Catholic Church*, #1235.

with the words, "In the Name of the Father, and of the Son, and of the Holy Spirit. Amen."

The sign is meant to solicit faith even in the face of difficult doubts. What is visible and physical is established in relation to what is invisible and spiritual. Tracing one's fingers from head to gut could be understood to indicate how our salvation extends from the highest to the most humble of human activities, from the most spiritual of powers of the soul to the very core of our bodily existence.[26] As we touch from one shoulder and cross over to the other, it is as if we are declaring the power of our faith extends out to everything that is within the horizon of humanity to master, command, possess, influence, protect and love.

left holds soldiers should right is the sword

The Summer of Violence

The Sign of the Cross can easily be an empty gesture if we do not choose to humble our hearts in a manner commensurate with what this sign signifies. When we do this, when we make the Sign of the Cross as an act of faith, the power of God echoes in our prayer, rooting it in the truth, making of it something that is pleasing to God.

This was experienced in a powerful way in the parish where I worked as we prepared for World Youth Day. In the weeks before the great occasion, the media in Denver dubbed the summer of '93, "the summer of violence." There were gang shootings that took the lives of many young people, not far from the boundaries of our parish. No one was sure what to do about the

---

[26] Olivier Clement describes three spiritual centers in the human person discussed by the Eastern Church Fathers: the *nous* or the mind, the seat of the intellect at the forehead, the *epithumus* or gut instincts, centered in the belly, and the *thumus* or the heart, the seat of tender affectivity where God speaks. See *The Roots of Christian Mysticism: Texts from the Patristic Era with Commentary*, trans. Theodore Berkeley and Hummerstone, New York: New City (1995, 7th printing 2002), 134.

situation or even how to pray about it, but our pastor, Fr. Marcian O'Meara, and several parishioners felt we must do something.

We decided to invite all the youth of the city to an evening of prayer. It was hoped that if young people prayed for peace, the Lord would bring peace back to the community. A Franciscan Friar, Fr. Stan Fortuna, c.f.r., came from New York to lead us in a holy hour. He and the other Franciscan Friars of the Renewal have worked for peace in *Fort Apache*, the Bronx, for years. Surely, he would be able to show our community how to pray.

Disappointingly, only a few young people and their families came for the event, but Fr. Stan was unperturbed by this turn-out. He began the evening simply by kneeling in the sanctuary before the Altar and the Cross. Making the Sign of the Cross, he cried out from his heart words which helped all of us configure ourselves to the sign we made with our hands, "Lord, have mercy on me and on everyone gathered here in prayer. We have been so indifferent to the plight of others. Now that violence touches our own community, who are we to dare to come before you and ask for your peace?"

With words to this effect, those of us at this vigil for peace suddenly saw the reality of our situation. When violence and suffering affected others, we were indifferent. Now, only when it affected us, did we come and ask the Lord for his peace. In other words, one of the reasons we did not have the peace of God in our community was that instead of going to God out of concern for the plight of others, we had for some time dared to approach Him with indifference, an indifference that impeded Him from pouring out His peace on us.

Fr. Stan helped us see our own coldness of heart and need for conversion. He helped us begin to pray from the place we really were. Those few who participated in this event remembered this prayer when, during and after World Youth Day, there was a dramatic decrease in crime and violence across the city. The power of Fr. Fortuna's words flowed from the Foot of the Cross, under the Sign of the Cross.

These many years later, I would like to think that the grace we received at the prayer vigil at Good Shepherd Parish secured God's protection against the evils that threatened us, but it is not that simple. Upon writing this, I am mindful of the innocent people massacred in a theatre in Aurora and still moved by the stories of those young people who sacrificed their lives to protect their loved ones. I cannot help but think of the bravery of those who responded to terrorist attacks in New York, Washington D.C. and on the flight over Pennsylvania. My memory also goes to Columbine High School and the innocent young people who were terrorized, martyred, and senselessly killed by their own peers.

Prayer is not magic but it is cruciform. Rooted in this world, it reaches for the heavens while embracing all manner suffering. The irrational brutality that has become a social affliction requires more than simply expressing a wish to the Lord. Violent outbursts of social rage are an occasion to be pierced to the heart, to reach out to those who need us, to turn to God and to allow Him to question us in prayer. The answer to violence is the Cross of Christ.

The Seal of our Heart

The Fathers of the Church called the Sign of the Cross a *seal*, and we could add it is like a "seal of the heart" (*Canticle of Canticles* 8:6). In fact, the action forms a cross over our whole body in the center of which is our heart. The heart is not only a physiological center of life for our body, but it speaks to a spiritual center of our very being.

The Sign of the Cross marks the deepest center of our personal existence. The deepest truth of the human being is that he is created in love, for love and by love. That is why the love ex-

56

pressed in the Sign of the Cross is the only appropriate seal for the heart.

The Sign of the Cross reminds us that the Living God has chosen to dwell with us in the substance of our soul. For those who seek to live in the peace of the Lord, the Sign of the Cross indicates the very threshold to this innermost sanctuary. It even more wonderfully signifies the overflowing fountain of mercy that Christ's death has enabled to gush forth from there.

The heart is a place of tender love. Only the heart that loves tenderly can welcome the heart of another. The Sign of the Cross means we have been welcomed into the Heart of Christ. It also means we welcome Christ into our hearts. He wants a real relationship with us. This is the reason that the Lord fashioned into being the substance of our soul.

When we rejected His love by sin, He did not want this innermost sanctuary of humanity to perish. But we would perish because we had rejected the very reason for our existence. Thus, He offered His heart to us on the Calvary, allowing it to be pierced by our unfaithfulness.

To be sealed with His love means to allow our hearts to be pierced by Him, by his faithfulness. When our hearts are fully sealed with His love in this way, we are established in peace with God and ourselves. The Sign of the Cross signifies that our hearts belong to Christ in this way.

Under the Sign of the Cross, we glimpse the possibilities of what the ancient monks meant by *habitare secum*, or living with oneself in solitude with the Lord. This involves the capacity to humbly welcome the Word of the Father into one's heart. It means to render the heart vulnerable to jubilation, a fullness of joy that compels one to respond to the great things God has done with one's whole existence. It is most properly in this context that *habitare secum* also refers to deliberation over how to respond to the Lord's invitation out of the depths of one's own being.

Those who want to pray must go there: every good, true and noble love is conceived in those depths before it is given birth in words and actions. All manner of wickedness is also conceived there and constantly threatens to overthrow the greatness of human dignity – and our prayer must also learn to submit this darkness to the Lord as well.

The Cross of Christ in this case points to and safeguards what is most tender and good about our humanity. This is true even in the face of our interior poverty and weakness. By crossing ourselves we signify the victory of good over evil that is accomplished there, and we do so with the hope that the work God has begun in us might reach completion.

A Sign in a World of Signs

Is this bodily action really so important for our life of prayer? The profound and mysterious relationships between body and soul, physical gesture and spiritual contemplation, the exterior day-to-day affairs of human life and the internal spiritual truths that sustain it converge. Making this Sign is important because we live in a world of meaning where signs, analogy, harmony and mediation all matter.

St. Athanasius describes this sign as an action of faith which opens up a true contemplation of the world. In the face of the evils afflicting this life, it takes faith to believe that God is almighty and concerned about our plight. Most of the time, faith alone sees the triumph of good over evil. Through this sign, bodily gesture disposes to this spiritual faith. He says that through this action the eye of faith raises its vision, from this visible world below to the heavens above, and in doing so renews our awareness of the victory of the Risen Lord over the powers of sin and death.[27]

---

[27] See *On the Incarnation*, 31 and 32.

Not only does the Cross lead us within ourselves but we also call it to mind because it defines our relationships with one another. Revealing who we are before God and the world, this sign reminds us to stand firm in our faith. When we make the Sign of the Cross we affirm our ecclesial identity as members of the Body of Christ, part of a people who find themselves at a crossroads, who have the opportunity to turn back to God.

By this Sign, we remember we must die to our wounded earthly desires so that we may live by Christ. The Sign of the Cross we make over our own bodies reminds us to offer our bodies for building up the Body of Christ. Making this Sign is also a constant reminder that we are in the world, but not of it: rejected, misunderstood, and persecuted, the Mystery of the Cross invoked by this simple gesture binds Christians to love even their enemies with gentle kindness and to work for the salvation of all.

The Sacred Bond between God and the Christian

The Sign of the Cross is a blessing, a sacramental.[28] When we say that the Sign of the Cross is a sacramental, we mean it expresses a renewal of that sacred bond established by Christ between the believer and God. As a sacramental, this sign binds us to liturgy, our holy service before the Lord.

The term "sacramental" like the word "sacrament" derives from the Latin, *sacramentum.* Originally, this word indicated the sacred oath by which the ancient Romans bound themselves in service to one another. Such agreements were based in a shared conviction about the value of piety and loyalty.

The Church in the West took up this term to translate and interpret the Greek word *mysterion.* The Biblical idea of mystery refers to invisible, spiritual power. Such a mystery is defined by a hidden wisdom and secret identity that the Lord entrusts to his disciples. In the Mystery of Christ they are adopted sons of the

---

[28] See *Catechism of the Catholic Church,* ##1078 and 1671.

Father. To live out this *sacramentum*, this *mysterion*, is to be plunged into a deep intimacy with Christ.

This special relationship with the Christ allows the Lord to lift up our humanity, not only out of sin, but also above itself. Christian prayer is ordered to something beyond this earthly existence, not in some remote moment in the future, but already right now, in the present moment. We, however, do not possess the power to realize this on our own. Only the Lord can give this power. How does He do this? This is where the use of signs comes into Christian prayer.

To understand the use of Christian signs in prayer, it is important to understand what Christ communicates through them. To raise us up above our nature and to bind us to God in love, the Risen Lord communicates His own life to us. The gift of participating in the life of Christ is called sanctifying grace. This is a divine gift that Christ won for us on the Cross. With this grace, we are made holy with the holiness of God.

We believe that Christ uses signs of faith to communicate this new life. During his ministry, Christ instituted signs in which He is objectively present working in the signs themselves: the Seven Sacraments. Because of the way He is present in the sacraments, it is perilous to receive them without the proper disposition. Of these sacraments, one stands out as the source and summit of the Church life – the Eucharist.

In the Eucharist, Christ is truly present by a special presence the Church calls "real." We believe that the bread and wine He blessed the night before He died are truly His Body and the Blood, the Soul and Divinity offered for our sake. The meaning of this paschal offering and the covenant it establishes is revealed and sealed by His death on the Cross. What is more, we believe He makes this offering of Himself truly present to us through the ministry of the priest at every mass. When we receive communion with right devotion, we truly enter this paschal mystery so that Christ's real presence roots us in Him. In this way, the Christ's

Eucharist will animate the Church with new life until the end of time.

Other liturgical signs complement this Eucharistic presence of Christ by directing us to the right attitude of heart. They are called sacramentals. The Sign of the Cross is one such sign. The Church instituted these signs to help us find the devotion we need to welcome the Lord's saving presence in the Eucharist and the other sacraments, and to strengthen our faith at other times as well.

Although they are distinct, it would be a serious mistake to fail to see the relationship between sacraments and sacramentals. The rituals for each of the Sacraments make use of all kinds of sacramentals. These sacramentals include sacred gestures, like the Sign of the Cross, as well as many other blessed images and objects.

Sacramentals of whatever kind find their source and summit in the Eucharist. Through this connection, Christ's gift of Himself at Mass is called to mind in all circumstances and situations. This means that the Sign of the Cross can extend the grace of Holy Communion in the here and now of this or that particular situation in which we find ourselves, no matter what it is.

The point is that when a baptized person performs an act of worship with living faith, like the Sign of the Cross, the whole liturgical dimension of his existence is unleashed. When this happens, the Christian has his love for the Lord enkindled. The frequent renewal of these holy affections for the Lord helps the spiritual life.

The Sign of the Cross also has a special connection to baptism. In fact, it refers to a renewal our baptismal promises. These are promises to reject all forms of evil and to believe in the Holy Trinity. The Sign of the Cross renews this solemn commitment. Ending with "Amen," a declaration of truth before God,[29] we re-

---

[29]See *Catechism of the Catholic Church*, ##1061 – 1065.

61

new our pledge of devotion to Him, and acknowledge that He is devoted to us even more.

A Sign of Protection

The saints use the Sign of the Cross as a shield, a protection against all evil, all diabolical irrationality. As she grew into spiritual maturity through prayer, St. Teresa of Avila came to understand the importance of this Sign. In fact, the first part of her *Interior Castle* suggests that if we do not enter more deeply into our hearts by disciplined prayer, we are unnecessarily vulnerable to anti-human spiritual forces. She describes such forces as poisonous snakes, toads and lizards which are always trying to frighten us away from a true encounter with the Lord.

Her point is that irrational forces are constantly trying to undermine our faith. She advocates making the Sign of the Cross as a sure way to stand firm against their attacks on our trust in God. Apparently, the physical action has spiritual power to deepen our confidence in such times of trial.

Going back even further, St. Anthony of the Desert, a 3rd Century Egyptian hermit, also encouraged the Sign of the Cross. He used the Sign of the Cross to combat all kinds of confusion, terror, deception, depression, frustration, nostalgia, discouragement, contention and a long list of other vexations that often haunt those who take up the battle to pray.[30] Dehumanizing irrationality is rendered powerless when exposed to the divine rationality of God's love revealed in the Cross.

The ancient forces that oppose what is genuinely human are in fact irrational and are powerless in the face of the truth. That is why they always work on the level of deception – misrep-

---

[30] See Athanasius, *Life of Anthony and the Letter to Marcellinus*, translation and Introduction by Robert C. Gregg, *Classics of Western Spirituality: A Library of Great Spiritual Masters*, editor Kevin A. Lynch C.S.P, Mahwah, N.J.: Paulist Press (1980), 41 and 48.

resenting the facts to confuse, seduce and discourage. Their objective is to rob humanity of its trust in God; for without trust in God's love, even recent history proves humanity is subject to every irrational impulse.

In the face of this, the Sign of the Cross indicates the truth of God's love for humanity and the greatness of human dignity that flows from this love. When the Christian mindfully crosses himself with faith, he not only calls to mind the great truth of his existence, he also grounds himself in the reason we have to trust God. A soul grounded in such trust and rooted deeply in the truth can be tried by all kinds of malicious falsehood, but as long as it remains under the Sign of the Lord's victory, it can never be overcome.

In the Age of Chivalry, St. Dominic would also arm himself with the Sign of the Cross before any prayerful study of the Bible or the Fathers of the Church. To prayerfully study the Word of God requires that we enter into a battle for the truth where thoughts opposed to God can sometimes assail us. He seems to have known that prayer without the Cross of Christ had its dangers. He was protecting himself.

When we go to pray, there are dehumanizing forces that want to oppose us and discourage our efforts. It seems, for St. Dominic, simply making the Sign of the Cross protected him from any suggestion that prayer was a waste of time, or something he could put off until later, or else something to become proud over. These kinds of thoughts are, after all, demonic ideas, ideas in direct opposition to the reality of prayer. Sometimes, he would repeat the gesture over and over as if he were swatting flies.[31]

---

[31] See Early Dominicans Selected Writings, Editor Fr. Simon Tugwell O.P., *Classics of Western Spirituality: A Library of Great Spiritual Masters*, editor Kevin A. Lynch C.S.P., Mahwah, N.J.: Paulist Press (1982), 101-102.

The Sign of Courage

For most Christians, especially the persecuted and those who are facing death, the Sign of the Cross is an occasion of hope and a source of strength. It is the sign of their forefathers in the faith—of men and women who courageously accepted persecution, rejection, imprisonment, torture and even death. When we make this sign, we also join ourselves to these holy men and women who went before us. We even enjoy a certain kind of solidarity with them in their sacrifice to God. Their complete trust in the Holy Trinity, all the way to the end, helps us to see that the truth of God's love is worthy of our lives. Thus, we too find the courage to accept this blessing and to stand firm in our faith.

Cardinal Nguyen Van Thuan while Archbishop of Saigon turned prisons in Vietnam into places of hope not only for his fellow prisoners but also for his guards. The Communists tried to break him by torturing and tormenting him. He endured nine years of solitary confinement in his thirteen years of prison. Humiliated, mocked, threatened, beaten - sometimes it was difficult for him to utter even simple vocal prayers. Yet he was never overcome.

He kept extending the hand of forgiveness and friendship to his tormentors. He never failed to find ways to encourage his fellow inmates. In the most difficult situations, Christ crucified gave him all he needed and he learned to rely on Him alone. By keeping his eyes on the Lord, he understood that he was on a journey even in prison, and that the trail he was blazing was a road to hope. The secret of his strength is found in the Sign of the Cross:

> Take as your wisdom the science of the cross (cf. 1 Cor.
> 2:2). Look to the cross; there you will find the solution to
> all the problems that worry you. If the cross is the stand-

ard by which you make your choices and decisions, your soul will be at peace.[32]

Making the Sign of the Cross involves the decision to choose the Cross of Christ as one's standard in life. The Sign is a reminder that every decision and action ought to be a response to the love the Lord revealed on the Cross. This love is a true sacrificial love, and to respond one must be ready to make real sacrifices of love in the circumstances of one's life. In the face of this reality, all one's actions are endowed with a spiritual meaning.

The gestures made with the body, one's actions, one's movements of heart, all of this is either an acceptance or rejection of the love expressed in the Sign of the Cross. Thus, when we make this Sign not only with our hand but also our heart and our mind, we involve our whole being in prayer. In this way, Christian prayer is meant to be profoundly whole – body and soul, affection and thought, heart and understanding. Such prayer leads to courage, the movement toward reconciliation with God, the beginning of a pilgrimage to our Father's house.

---

[32] *The Road of Hope: a gospel from prison*, trans. Peter Bookallil, Boston: Pauline Books and Media (2001) 227.

Chapter Four

Prayer is a Journey,
a Pilgrimage of Love

St. John of the Cross, a master poet and a man of profound intimacy with God, was very busy with all kinds of administrative duties as a reformer of the Carmelite Order while He directed hundreds of souls in spiritual life. For his generosity with God and desire to promote contemplation, he was blessed with imprisonment, humiliation, rejection and all kinds of persecution.

The Carmelite Master describes God's mysterious love towards humanity in terms of human love. The natural experience of falling in love is analogous to the beginning of the spiritual life. Romantic love starts with a passionate desire for the beloved. The spiritual life also begins with a restless need to find God.

St. John of the Cross connects these experiences throughout his poetry. He is fascinated with the soul that longs with an ardent affection to be with the Lord. To bring this out, he begins his *Spiritual Canticle* with soul's cry to God: "Where have you hidden?"

This question speaks to spiritual awakening. Only a heart awakened by the Lord becomes alive with this anxious desire. Many who are drawn to begin the life of prayer mistakenly believe that they are the ones who have initiated a relationship with God. The actual situation is just the opposite.

Until the Lord rouses us, it is possible to drift through life indifferent to His great love. We remain under the sway of earthly dreams. If we are not awakened from these fantasies, they will destroy us. This is because human existence needs the greatness of the truth. This is why the Bridegroom comes for us, to give us the fullness of truth, the truth about love.

The Bridegroom initiates the spiritual life but He expects us to apply ourselves in vigilantly seeking Him. When we first begin to seek Him, we cannot easily find Him. St. John of the Cross explains that He is hidden in the substance of our faith and if we are to ever find Him we must enter into this hidden secret as well.

We enter into this hidden secret by pulling ourselves together and focusing our attention on the Lord with trust. Crossing this threshold into silence involves the effort to entrust all concerns to the Lord because a soul distracted with anxieties is not free to enjoy friendship with God. This time spent searching for the Lord in the secret of faith welcomes the presence of Someone who awaits us in love.

The Beauty of the Soul

Saint John of the Cross teaches that God is more present to the soul than the soul is to itself. By this presence, God holds each life, every person, in existence. As remarkable as this is, the Carmelite Doctor also holds that such an intimate presence of God does not preclude even more captivating forms of His presence.

These astonishing ways God chooses to be present in the heart are supernatural and relational. God, according to the unfathomable wisdom of His divine plan, has elected to dwell in us as a friend who is known and loved. Because He loves us excessively, He is always disclosing Himself in some new way. Each new discovery of His surprising presence has the nature of a gift, a sheer grace that we have done nothing to deserve.

Humbly accepting this gift with grateful trust is the only proper response to such divine generosity. To trust God is to live vulnerable to the gentle confession of His love. His desire for our friendship pierces into the deepest center of our innermost being.

It is by going into those beautiful depths that we learn to love the Lord whose tender concern for us is the source of our beauty.

This journey where faith is led by love to love has been known by many names: prayer of the heart, mental prayer, silent prayer. Those who accept this gift of prayer know that the most powerful presence of God is encountered, not in the things we do, but in the depths of who we are. His love defines us.

It is on this point that St. John of the Cross pleads with his readers to spend their prayer seeking the presence of the Lord within. Just as Jesus declares that "the kingdom of God is within" and St. Paul asserts, "You are the temple of the Holy Spirit," John of the of the Cross passionately affirms, "Oh, then, soul, most beautiful among all creatures, so anxious to know the dwelling place of your Beloved so you may go in search of Him and be united with Him, now we are telling you that you yourself are His dwelling and His secret inner room and hiding place."[33]

The deepest reality of the human heart is that it is a sacred sanctuary meant for God, a place where He can be loved, known and served – a place where He loves, knows, and serves the work of his Hands. Union with God is not about being absorbed into an abstract absolute, rather it is about entering into a real relationship, a tender friendship with the Lord.

The heart provides a spiritual space for God and man to be together, to relate in personal friendship. We have been mysteriously fashioned to bear the constant transforming impact of the Lord's limitlessness on our limitedness. Rather than crushing us in our weakness, this divine encounter is exactly what makes us more fully human and more wholly alive.

St. Augustine of Hippo speaks of the Lord entering his heart as if entering a house. He says the house is too small and cluttered, but he is confident the Lord can clean it and make it

---

[33] *Spiritual Canticle*, 1:7 in *Collected Works of St. John of the Cross*, trans. Kieran Kavanaugh and Otilio Rodriguez, Washington, D.C.: ICS (1991), 480.

larger.[34] The events of his life to which he bears witness in his *Confessions* suggest that Augustine spent time in prayer probing his memory to find God's mercy in the face of his own misery. Teresa of Avila advocates the same practice: Beginners in prayer must accustom themselves "to thinking about their past life" which can be painful, "for they do not fully understand whether or not they are repentant for their sins."[35]

Beautiful Encounters of the Heart

There are beautiful encounters with God waiting for each of us in the human heart. He is the question that makes our lives unbearably restless and the answer in which alone we find our peace. He speaks as the most interior voice appealing to what is right, confirming what is good and admonishing what is wrong. He is the source and summit of everything that is good, noble and true about the human person. He is the conqueror and destroyer of anything that is evil, ignoble and false. He is the mirror in which we find reflected all the ways we have compromised ourselves. He is reflected in the treasured propositions of our faith that the heart must guard.

Sometimes He waits for us in memories. He often reveals something of Himself in a conversation with a friend.   He can sneak up and surprise us in a moment of solitude where the immensity of creation moves us to pray. Other times, He is found patiently bearing the painful wounds left behind by our self-indulgence or insobriety. Sometimes we must search for the Lord in those heartaches wherein even those we most trusted betrayed or abandoned us.

---

[34] See *Confessions*, Book 1.v.
[35] *The Book of Her Life*, 11.9, *Collected Works of St. Teresa of Avila*, vol. 1, trans. Kieran Kavanaugh and Otilio Rodriguez, Washington, D.C: ICS (1976, 2nd edition revised 1987) 114.

As we descend into such places of our lives, we find ourselves enveloped in a sober silence where the truth about one's life can suddenly sting. Where this truth stings the most is where God is most present. He has let this truth sting Him, too. Faith led by love alone sees the One who made Himself vulnerable to our heartaches.

Most people suffer the experience of the Lord's absence while they are still learning to seek Him by faith. We will explore the purpose of this difficult experience later in our chapter on the spiritual nights our pilgrimage of faith passes through. In the context of the beauty of the soul, it is enough for us to recall that the soul is more than the operations of its psychological faculties and what is experienced or not experienced.

St. John of the Cross wants us to know that journey of faith takes us beyond anything the imagination or the intellect or the passions attain by their own operation. This means that prayer is a matter of turning one's attention to the Lord even when nothing can be imagined, or thought, or even felt about Him. When the Lord is hidden like this, He is finally free to enter our lives on His own terms and we are finally free to rely on His limitless love rather than our own limited efforts.

St. John of the Cross's *Spiritual Canticle* describes different kinds of messengers and messages. The Bridegroom communicates His heart-piercing love in these many ways to ever more deeply wound the heart with wonder. A love-sick heart finds its way more eagerly and cannot be daunted by trials and hardships. To be drawn, to be attracted, and to be captivated by the Lord is the very source of the spiritual life. The more He draws us to Himself, the easier it is to find Him.

Messengers the Lord Sends

St. John of the Cross explains that there are different kinds of messages and messengers the Lord sends us.[36] The messages

---

[36] *Spiritual Canticle*, 7.

and the messengers themselves are the Lord's attempt to reach us where we are. The messengers include everything He has clothed in beauty and virtue in creation.[37]

Whether visible or invisible, physical or spiritual, Christ can speak through the beauty of it: sunsets, forests, babies, preachers and even the super-intelligent extraterrestrial beings we call angels. All these messengers rise up together in a symphony of truth proclaiming Him. St. Augustine, whose thought anticipates the Spanish Doctor nicely on this point, observes, "All about me, heaven and earth, and everything that is in them, proclaim that I should love you, and their message never ceases to sound."[38]

Each message that comes through God's messengers deepens our longing for the Lord. St. John of the Cross describes this longing for the Lord as a kind of wound of the heart. He has in mind the kind of love that wounds a lover the closer He draws to his beloved. One might think of how the messages of Cyrano de Bergerac gradually wound Roxanne more and more, deepening her love and yearning for her beloved.

The longing God produces in one's heart can be of greater or lesser intensity and duration depending on the kind of message He sends, and our openness. It is really our own fault if we are not open and prepared. God politely communicates only the messages for which we are ready as we progress deeper into the mystery of His love.

In the end, the messages are not enough to satisfy the soul. The soul hungers for something more, something the messengers cannot give. Souls who reach this point in their journey or prayer glimpse distant horizons to which the messengers can only point. Here, the real reason God sent the messengers is laid bare—He has made us for Himself and we cannot rest until we rest in Him.[39]

---

[37] *Spiritual Canticle*, 6.

[38] *Confessions*, Book 10. 6, trans. R.S. Pine-coffin, Penguin Books: New York, (1961), 211.

[39] See St. Augustine, *Confessions*, 1.1.

The Beauty of Creation

The first kind of messenger the Lord sends are all the different kinds of creatures and works that compose the beauty of visible reality. Our contemporary gaze is too dull and banal. We do not see the multiplicity of creation signifying the excessiveness of God's love for us.

The only meaning of material things we often entertain is exhausted by our ability to manipulate or consume them. The vast multitude of messengers bursting into the present moment remains impenetrable to eyes blinded by such opportunism. For our own lack of wonder, the divine love letter, which visible creation tries to share with us in spectacularly tangible ways, is often left unread.

Ignorance concerning the sacred purpose of creation, however, does not completely prevent the beauty of nature from conveying the message entrusted to it. Even souls furthest from God are occasionally enchanted: the glowing embers of a sunset, the crashing surf against coastline, the gentle whisper of the wind rolling across the plains, the magical starlight that from time to time twinkles on even the most polluted of cities. As we begin to pray, the Lord helps us to become more sensitive to such beauty.

Gerald Manley Hopkins' poem *God's Grandeur* presents how God's glory in creation flames out and gathers to greatness even in a world abused by men. It is a great grace to see with this poet in the living of freshness of each morning the radiant wings and brooding presence of the Holy Spirit.

The reality is that, from the beauty of the smallest insect to the faint shining lights of the furthest stars of the furthest galaxy, the whole visible cosmos constitutes God's declaration of love to the whole of humanity, and His particular affection for each person individually. This radiant form of creation as a whole confirms Fyodor Dostoevsky's observation that beauty will save the world.[40]

How do we vigilantly attend to such a message? St. Augustine suggests a method for listening to what visible creation has to tell us. Question these things with our heart as we behold them and they say something to us. In other words, our natural sense of wonder at what is visibly manifest before us disposes us to something God wants to communicate. He suggests that when we gaze on the things God has made, their beauty speaks to us:

> I spoke to all the things that are about me, all that can be admitted by the door of the senses, and I said, 'Since you are not my God, tell me about Him. Tell me something of my God.' Clear and loud they answered, 'God is He who made us.' I asked these questions simply by gazing at these things, and their beauty was all the answer they gave.[41]

God's visible creatures communicate to us spiritual realities all the time because visible creation is a gift to humanity and this gift is designed to point to the Giver. The message of visible creation, when we are open, produces a longing for God in us, a natural religious sense of things. Blessed Elisabeth of the Trinity shared this conviction. For her, all of creation is a kind of sacrament, something that gives us God.

Consider one's own heartbeat: drawing all the body's blood to itself and then sending it out to the body's furthest reaches. In this sense, each heartbeat is an incredible gift for which to

---

[40] See his novel *The Idiot*, trans. Constance Garnett (New York: Bantam, 1981), 370.
[41] *Confessions*, Book 10.6, trans. R.S. Pine-coffin, Penguine Books: New York, (1961), 212.

praise God on many different levels. Through the heartbeat, we begin to see that God is the Author of Life, *all life*.

At the same time, the heartbeat spiritually signifies what God continually does for those He loves. By a movement of His heart He draws us close to Him in the deepest kind of friendship and communion.[42] By another movement He sends us out into the world so that everyone (our friends, yes even our enemies) might not perish, but that they might have eternal life.

A mind searching for God in prayerful silence often finds itself caught in the wonder of the things He has made. Everything, even in a beat of the heart, is like a sacrament that communicates the love of God. Sometimes the mind awash in wonder discovers itself submerged in adoration, and astounded by the splendor of the Lord, it bows in humble silence.

This kind of message, whenever we receive it, explains St. John, wounds us with a light wound. This means that although such a message of love actually scrapes our heart, the scratch goes away after a while. We might remember an experience of this kind from time to time, but like a scratch the wonder that filled us was not enough to change our hearts.

Such scrapes are not sufficient for lasting union with God or deep spiritual transformation. Instead, they make us vulnerable to more intimate communications from the Lord. Though our heart is only briefly stung by these messages, the visible beauty of creation encourages us to desire and to seek God more and more, and never to lose heart.

There are messages the Lord sends to us that go beyond encouragement. They are transformative because they open us in deeper ways to the life of Christ. These words of love, because of

---

[42] Probably the most beautiful description of this is to be found in Hans Urs von Balthasar's *Heart of the World*. He takes readers on a meditation on time and eternity, the paschal mystery and the restlessness of God's heart for humanity – a sort of inversion of St. Augustine's *Confessions*.

their quality and intensity, leave deeper wounds than the messages sent through visible creation.

The Words of a Preacher

Besides speaking to us through natural, visible wonders, the Lord also speaks to us through people and angels. Rational creatures know and communicate what they know with intentionality, with purpose. Again, the Living God longs to disclose himself and in this case, He has chosen to do so through others.

This means that none of the people God has placed in your life are there accidentally. They are there to teach you something about the Lord. Sometimes they do this through their good actions. Oftentimes they do this through the ways they hurt us. But whether they do ill or good, God is revealing Himself to us through them and we need to think about what He is saying.

Among people, the Lord prefers the lowly and poor for his most important messages. This is why those beginning to pray must heed the exhortation of Blessed Teresa of Calcutta to seek Christ in the distressing disguise of the poor. While many look at poverty as a problem to be solved, Mother Teresa understood that each of those suffering from hunger and abandonment are a blessing entrusted to us by God: each one deserving not only to be relieved and consoled, but welcomed and treasured. The reality is that through the poor, Jesus shares a message that pierces to the heart. He, in fact, is counting on us, hoping in us far more than we could ever hope in Him.

If anyone knows the Lord, it is because the Lord sent someone to share the Gospel with that person: sometimes by words, often by actions and hopefully by both. If at the time nothing happened, that person planted a seed that the Lord would let sprout later. In beginning to pray, it is important from time to time to call to mind the messengers the Lord has sent into our lives and what it is they witnessed to. When we do this, beginning to pray comes easily.

St. John of the Cross describes the wound that comes when we hear the Gospel and embrace the truths of the faith men and angels share with us. He calls it a festering wound. What he means is that this kind of wound does not easily go away. It moves us to change our lives, to begin to pray.

Maybe we were praying before, but when we hear the words of the Gospel, a truth pierces our hearts that makes us want to continue to be disciplined in our prayer, to make prayer part of our everyday life. To open our hearts to this kind of wound means we need to open our minds to the doctrine of the Church. The teaching of the Church is revealed in the Scriptures and Tradition. Those wanting to make good progress in prayer need to seek out strong catechesis, reliable counsel and good preaching.

Unfortunately, we live in a time when there still can be a lot of very poor preaching and weak catechesis. There are very few who have the spiritual gifts or the intellectual formation to provide solid counsel. This means that we need to carefully discern everything. Even good teachers err and bad preachers can sometimes get it right. But, how do we know? It is by their fruits that you know them.

Prayer rooted in sacred doctrine gives new life to our dying world. Solid teaching is the fertile soil of deep prayer. When the words of a preacher shake us up out of our spiritual slumber, when they give us courage in the face of sorrow, when they move us to purify ourselves, when they quicken our love for the Lord, when they implicate us in our neighbor's plight—we can easily discern the truth which gives life to prayer.

For my generation, there is a lack of trust in God and thus a narrow vision of what it means to listen to God and to cry to Him from the depths of one's being. Confusing catechesis and poor preaching have caused many to imagine prayer as powerless and anachronistic. Raising the heart and mind to God is not looked upon as having any real power to change one's own life, let alone the world.

Prayer is presumed at best therapeutic, one more form of mental hygiene. Most do not believe it is scientific enough, and because it is not scientific, it is therefore on the level of fantasy and myth. Because of this mentality, it is not uncommon to find Catholics turning to psychology, pharmaceutical drugs, magical thinking or commercialized meditation techniques to solve life's problems.

On the other hand, there are others who teach true doctrine, but they do this as if they were shadow boxing. They are so worried about the precision and correctness of their assertions; they forget that the message is not an end in itself. Sacred doctrine is supposed to lead to communion with God. This was a lesson that I learned the hard way.

When I first started to direct catechesis for the Rites of Christian Initiation at a parish in Colorado, I thought that an accurate presentation of the doctrine of the Church was sufficient for conversion. Those who went through this program acquired head-knowledge about doctrine, but what they were learning with their intellects was not always penetrating the heart.

My approach was not entirely wrong. The truths of the faith are truth-bearing: God himself is encountered when we choose to believe them. My error was that I believed if catechumens knew the content of the faith with a clear and comprehensive understanding, they would necessarily encounter the Lord.

What I discovered, however, was many who took these classes left the Church after only a few years. They needed more than facts, more than familiarity with the truths of the faith. They needed to personally encounter the Truth Himself and fall in love with Him. I failed to teach them how to really pray.

The mind is the battlefield of the heart. Christians are called to be worshippers both in spirit and truth. We will never hit the target if we remain either too sentimental or too abstract or both. Doctrine without prayer lacks heart. Prayer without sound teaching degenerates to pious sentimentality. Hopefully, a new wave of theologians will come to unlock the riches of the Western tradition of prayer for our contemporaries. They will teach the truth so that people will find God.

Anytime anyone warms our heart to the Lord, stirs us with gratitude for what God has done, leads us to sorrow over our indifference to his love; such a person is a messenger from God. These messengers are not always human. It is a consolation to realize that some of those beautiful thoughts that pop out of nowhere might not have been the product of our own limited imagination or cleverness. An Angel of God might have preached to us and we did not even know it. They are subtle beings after all.

On the other hand, if someone's words disturb or distract us from prayer, even if they quote the Scriptures, God might still speak through them but it will be despite their teachings and not because of them. Preachers and teachers need to be steeped in prayer and sound doctrine. Their lives must be commensurate with the message with which God has entrusted them.

The Word Himself

There is one more kind of message that St. John of the Cross calls a mortal wound. Those who experience this kind of communication from the Lord feel like they are dying of love. Their earthy existence cannot contain the intensity of desire for God burning in their hearts. In a certain sense, they become dead to this present life.

All the great and marvelous things of this world no longer have a grip on their heart, and they live, no longer for those things, but for the Lord who made them. They long to be satisfied by the Lord and they are convinced that He alone can fulfill the deepest desires of their hearts. These deep desires begin to drive their life in a new way.

The Carmelite mystic explains that this kind of wound is not caused by doctrine itself, but something beyond the ideas and construct of that doctrine. The actual words of the preacher are received like so much stammering, because the soul is no longer attentive to them. It is resting in something deeper.

Preaching opens up a contemplation of revealed truth which takes up the highest level of human consciousness while also rendering us receptive to mystical wisdom. The scientific study of divine revelation can sometimes be merely an intellectual game taken up for its own enjoyment or to impress others. This, however, is an abuse of its true purpose. True theology endeavors to direct humanity to the reason for our hope – and sometimes the reason we discover no words can express.

Theology is meant to be like a window through which God shines on us. It is a study we carry out on our knees. Sacred doctrine is meant to bear the speech of God who has spoken everything to us in the Word made flesh. When by a beautiful movement of grace we hear His voice in our contemplation of what He has revealed, our hearts become immovably established in the Truth Himself.

This is the eternal Word spoken by the Father into our humanity—the greatest and most definitive message of all. No earthly language can adequately express its mystery and yet every tongue must confess its glory. Those who have received this Word of the Father only want to live by love, for love and in love: the love of Christ has pierced them so deeply they have died to everything else.

You are a Temple of the Holy Spirit

To illustrate what it is like to encounter the Word Himself through the stammering of a preacher, there is a wonderful story about Blessed Elisabeth of the Trinity. She felt an overwhelming presence of God dwelling in her heart when she prayed He flooded her with such intense love she felt it was excessive.

The catechesis of the time, like our own, was very poor. At the time, many catechists and preachers emphasized God's displeasure with humanity over sin. So her experience and her catechesis did not match up. In an effort to gain some clarity, she decided to seek out the counsel of a wise old priest from the Order of Preachers.

Père Vallée, O.P. was a spiritual director and preacher for the convent she would later join. As she related her experience, he understood what the Lord was doing. Quoting St. Paul, he asked the teenager, "Do you not know that you are a temple of the Holy Spirit?"

What she knew in prayer was validated in an instant and she became open to an even deeper intimacy with the Lord. Her prayer took her completely out of herself and wholly into God's presence. The priest saw that she was not listening anymore even as he continued his teaching. What he had to say was in harmony with her experience, but what she was encountering was something even more than what could be said.

Drawing from theology of St. Thomas Aquinas, the Dominican attempted to elucidate the indwelling of the Trinity and how it increases the more open we are to the grace of God.[43] The Holy Trinity dwells in our hearts to be loved and adored by grace. In an earlier chapter, we referred to grace is a participation in the life of the Trinity. This is the new life that flows through the Cross of Christ into the depths of our being. This new life makes us Christ-like and the more Christ-like we are; the more God is present in new and wonderful ways.

In a certain sense, the spiritual missions of the Spirit and the Son into the soul are ecstatic in character. These missions are part of the divine economy, the way the unchangeable God surmounts the abyss that yawns between Him and the wonders He

---

[43] See *Summa Theologica* I, q43, a.3-6.

has made. Because they are directed to the human heart, these divine missions enable the heart go out of itself and enter into God.

Every time our mind becomes more vulnerable to the glory of the Father through a word of truth, the Word of the Father gives Himself to be possessed in a new way by a deeper faith. Whenever our affectivity bursts into the warmth of devotion, this likeness to the Holy Spirit allows us to enjoy a deeper relationship with Him.

Because God is ineffable, the greater our likeness to the Son and the Spirit in these ways, the indwelling presence of the Holy Trinity can constantly extend and deepen so as to overflow our whole being. In other words, God's love is excessive: it exceeds all bounds. This introduces something ecstatic into our very substance.

The missions of the Son and the Spirit form us for a special purpose that the Father has for us. The divine missions form the Christian heart for mission. Christians are empowered to manifest a work of love so beautiful; the limits of this present life are not enough to express it all. In other words, the Trinity does not absorb us into absolute being. The Trinity relates to us in such a way that the more deeply related we are to this mystery, the more fully we become the creatures God intended us to be, creatures capable of participating in His mysterious plan of love.

Blessed Elisabeth's heart was turned to the Word who whispered to her over the priest's words. Fired by love's urgings, the words of a preacher would be reduced to stammering whenever the Word Himself touched her heart like that. In fact, making this excessive love of the Lord known to others would become her spiritual mission.

Although they are thought to be rare experiences, such messages are not extraordinary according to St. John of the Cross. When the Word of the Father touches the heart, the whole soul is completely captivated by Him, if only for a moment. Because this wisdom accesses such great depths of the heart, mere explanations about Lord no longer satisfy in the same way. It becomes ordinary for a heart initiated in this deeper wisdom to find satisfaction in the possession of Him alone.

Chapter Five

Secret Encounters in the Night

Progress in the journey of faith is made through new and unfolding encounters with Christ. Of the encounters in store for us in this life, the most beautiful and painful are those in the mysterious nights through which the soul must pass. Some of these nights are darker than others.

When the divine messengers come less frequently, when the consoling sense that God is near at hand disappears, when the heart aches to be with God who seems absent, the soul is already engulfed in night, a spiritual darkness in which it cannot find its way by itself. Paradoxically, this difficult darkness is a great blessing. In this night, we learn to let go of our own cleverness and allow the love that comes from God to guide our faith.

When God's Seems Absent

The most powerful experiences of God are those of which we are least aware. Although prayer begins when God in some way discloses His love for us, sooner or later the initial comfort this provided subsides. We begin to question whether what we experienced was real. St. John of the Cross sees in this common experience a crucial principle in Christian prayer at work.

In *Ascent of Mt. Carmel*, he explains that, although God is always present, we do not always *feel* or *sense* or *know* that we enjoy His presence. God's presence does not require our conscious awareness or our intuition or our affections or our imagination or our even thoughts. Instead, the Trinity who dwells in our hearts only requires faith fired by love.[44]

Faith is a night for the soul in which the Lord discloses Himself. There are times in marriage and religious life when we do not need to feel or understand love to make the decision to love, we only need to believe in it. This is what makes love strong. It is the same way in prayer. For St. John of the Cross, the opportunity to cleave to Jesus in no other way than by faith fired by love is a sheer grace. It is exactly this sheer grace he describes as the dark night.[45]

The metaphor of night offers a rich image for the role of faith in prayer. The image of night can evoke fear but it can also be enchanting.[46] The darkness of night is the friend of lovers who meet to exchange their pledges of love to one another under its shadow. Such intimacy does not belong to the outside world or the light of day. Similarly, the night of faith shelters the deep secrets we exchange in friendship with the Lord.

The dark night protects Christian prayer from spiritual gluttony. Such impulsiveness in prayer, even if involuntary, sets us on a path away from *conversatio morum.* That is, the whole manner of our life is not entirely vulnerable to the Author and Perfecter of our faith. When we are driven by the need for spiritual experience or satisfying results, the cold calculating light of human cleverness makes prayer vulnerable to all kinds of self-deception. One Camaldolese hermit explains it this way:

> The dominant spiritual climate manifests ... an extreme individualism. It is not so much God who is of interest to us, to speak with Him and to belong to Him, but rather we look for personal experience, we shut ourselves up in our

---

[44] See *Ascent of Mount Carmel*, book 2, chapters 1-2.
[45] See Dark Night, Book 1, 4-5.
[46] See Iain Matthews, *Soundings from St. John of the Cross: The Impact of God*, London: Hodder (1995) 51ff,

own spiritual search ...Let us admit that, at present, a spiritual self-centeredness reigns, which arises from the current opinion that the world is only an appearance and that, basically, the self and God coincide. If the supreme criterion of life in Christ is no longer adherence in faith to the Triune God, but personal experience, the change to a religious syncretism will be quickly made.[47]

We can add that extreme individualism drives a spiritual consumerism in our culture. For many, prayer is no more than one more product that promises euphoria, relief from stress, a sense of control or else a form of mental hygiene. According to this hermit, we get what we pay for.

He refers to syncretism. This is the patching together of religious practices and beliefs that appeal to our imagination and conform to our social preferences. Hubris prevents us from acknowledging the religious addiction driving this idolatry. It can only be magical thinking that keeps grasping for the next system or program with the same futile hope that, once the desired outcome is achieved, all will be well.

No anticipated outcome ever addresses what really ails us. Trying to grab onto someone's technique or method is to behave as victims of a drowning accident frantically pulling each other to ruin in the effort to survive. By itself, humanity is incapable of producing anything that can manage the reality of sin, its wounds or its consequences.

Under the weight of sin, the ego has its own specific gravity. Without God, nothing we produce—no program, no process, no technology—can get us beyond ourselves. Contemporary man for all his technological mastery needs a savior now every bit as much as has the rest of humanity all through history.

---

[47] *In Praise of Hiddeness: The Spirituality of the Camaldolese Hermits of Monte Corona,* Bloomingdale, OH: Ercam Editions (2007), 53

In the darkness of faith, love guides prayer to a spiritual space large enough for the Lord deal with the reality of sin and the misery it causes. Here is precisely where faith frees one from extreme individualism. Faith guided by love hears Christ asking us to give Him our misery that He might give us His glory.

Those who cry out in faith to Christ crucified are open to a whole world beyond the self, a world in which personal experience is measured against something greater than we can ask or imagine. This search for God rejects all forms of subjectivism. Whether there is enlightenment or only darkness, joy or sorrow, elation or suffering, the soul is always captivated by the Bridegroom, drawn by Him, even when it does not know it.

This kind of openness in prayer is Christian contemplation. It is listening to the Word of the Father. It is beholding the Light of the Word. In this Light, the world cannot be mistaken as a mere appearance that I surmount in my lust for the spiritual. Instead, everything in life, each moment, manifests God's glory so that I might learn to wonder and bow my humble existence before the immensity of His love.

Christians pray with the deep conviction that "the self" is not God. Nor do they believe it is an illusion. They see themselves in His image and likeness, and because of this, they do not dare seek to surmount themselves.

By contemplative prayer, they learn to accept the boundaries Divine Wisdom has established. In silent contemplation, they suffer just how different God is, even as He fills the whole substance of these souls with new meaning. The more they suffer this difference in prayer, the more they realize the divine likeness with which they were fashioned. His humble immensity creates in them an immense humility. Through this new creation, the self is finally free to prostrate in adoration as it was originally meant to—not for the sake of the experience, but for love.

To achieve this great work, God leads us beyond the initial comforts we felt in prayer. He wants to give us something so much more than what is merely comfortable. Only deep prayer searches the inexhaustible riches of his love. Even under the burden of catastrophic hardships, deep prayer carries us in the shadows of glory. We feel crushed but He is raising us up. We are wrapped in darkness, but love guides us through the night.

An Initial Glimpse of the Night

The first retreat I ever made was in a Camaldolese Hermitage in Big Sur, California. This part of the Central Coast towers up over the ocean with dangerous beauty. Though the hermitage is up high, if you listened carefully at night, you can hear the surf beating against the rocks far below. It is like the heartbeat of God.

This holy place is baptized in all kinds of silence. Daily Mass and the Liturgy of the Hours observed by the hermits only punctuate the quiet peace with even deeper silences. In fact, the whole experience was very soothing even if, as a high school freshman, I found the intensity of these silences difficult to endure.

I had been invited with a group of university students—all of whom felt an attraction to prayer and spirituality. A little uncomfortable socially, something was drawing me to enter into this experience with them. Having grown up in a household of seven brothers with lots of guests and relatives coming in and out, a whole weekend of silence presented an exotic opportunity.

Under that beautiful blanket of solitude, prayer was not easy. It was tedious. I spent most of my time reading and trying to listen to the Lord even while noisy thoughts kept distracting me. The Living God I sought was mysteriously hidden. I wanted a spiritual experience, but the Lord gave me something much more important. He gave a first taste of that *sheer grace* called *night*.

The pathway of prayer that began to unfold on that retreat is not one trod by following feelings or thoughts or religious fantasy. This is true even if along the way we do feel and think and imagine many wonderful things. This journey was not about a state of consciousness or any other psychological achievement - even if along the way all kinds of transforming and purifying moments can overtake our psychological faculties.

This many years later, it is easier to see that the Lord was using my fascination with silence and love for nature to draw me into a deeper relationship with Him. He was also beginning to show me that cleaving to the Word made flesh in faith is the only sure way to progress on the pathway of prayer. This journey is fired, not by experiences that please us, but by the holy desire to please the Lord. It is the way of vulnerability, complete openness to the love of God.

There are those who spend a lifetime availing themselves to the unfathomable workings of divine love. Those souls yearn to do something beautiful for God, and they feel the need to respond with all kinds of heroic resolutions, even to the taking up seeming impossible tasks, and this without ever counting the cost. Content with believing in the love that flows from an ongoing conversation with the Lord, they would not have it any other way.

The Dark Night and St. Faustina

This experience was especially strong for St. Faustina Kowalska whose conversion we described in the first chapter. She wanted to serve the Lord because she glimpsed how much He loved her. To prepare her for the mission that He would entrust her with, the Lord allowed her to suffering all kinds of physical hardships but also intense interior trials. Sometimes she appeared so desolate she looked inconsolably depressed. Although melancholy sometimes can be overwhelming for people of prayer for purely physiological reasons, her depression was related to what she felt as the Lord's absence when she tried to pray.

Every time she had a profound encounter with the Lord that especially consoled her, she eventually came to expect trials. Somehow the Lord's presence was meant to sustain her for the more difficult times. Interestingly enough, another saint began suffering this feeling of the Lord's absence at about the same time. The difference was that although St. Faustina's trials ended with her death at the age of 33, Blessed Mother Teresa of Calcutta's painful experiences of the dark night would last for decades.

For reasons only the Lord fully knows, He chooses sometimes not to allow us to feel Him. This feeling that the Lord is absent is not rooted in reality. Without God's presence we could not exist. Thus, the feeling that God is absent is only a feeling, but a very difficult one. God mysteriously permits souls to suffer this kind of trial for a very special purpose, sometimes for a very long time.

The Lord, when He allows a soul to suffer a sense of His absence, establishes our hearts in a kind of knowing that reaches deeper than any natural perceptions. Such loving knowledge is only possible by a love filled faith that hopes in God even when He seems most absent.

Spiritual Trials are a Necessary Part of Prayer

Spiritual trials are a common, yet daunting, experience for anyone truly dedicated to prayer. We have already explored one dimension of this experience in the life of St. Therese of Lisieux in our discussion on doubt. This experience is also thematic throughout the letters published by Mother Teresa's spiritual director in *Come Be My Light - The Private Writings of the Saint of Calcutta*. This same experience is a striking feature of Jean Bernard's autobiographical reflections in *Priestblock 25487: A memoir of Dachau* and Cardinal Nguyen van Thuan thoughts about his own imprisonment in *Testimony of Hope*. In other words, all great saints and holy people suffer trials. Spiritual hardship is somehow integral to the life of prayer.

Since God is always present sustaining the existence of all things, what explains this seeming absence, especially in those moments we most need Him in prayer? Earlier we proposed that these trials free us from extreme individualism and dispose us to go to the Lord by faith. When we think about this further, we come up against a very disconcerting fact: even very holy people undergo all kinds of trials and sometimes die in the midst of them. There is no nice neat cliché that addresses this well. The only answer is to be found in continuing to seek the One for whom we yearn even when it feels as if we have been abandoned.

Those who have suffered such things are often very sober about the freedom the Lord has to relate to us as He wills, when He wills, for His own purposes. Divine Providence is surprising, surpassing all expectation. In the face of this, they have learned to go to Him in humble trust, with empty hands, wholly vigilant for His Coming.

This does not mean that one should refrain from presenting the Lord heartfelt petitions regarding our concerns and needs. Crises, anxiety, and stress drive us to God. If He permits things to fall apart, it is because He wants us to realize we need Him more than we need anything else. Giving primacy to God's plan, trusting that He really is concerned about my concerns, (but in ways I do not always understand), all of this means patiently suffering what feels like complete abandonment while living by love.

Nights of Sense and of Spirit

The grace of Christ is manifold in the ways it challenges, questions, invites and convinces our hearts to trust in Him. John of the Cross teaches that there are many kinds of nights that one must pass through in our journey of faith. Of all the nights that there are to describe, he focuses on two: the Night of the Senses and the Night of the Spirit.[48]

Because we are created as embodied souls, there is both an exterior and interior dimension to our being. Our bodies, our senses, our imagination, our tastes, our inclinations pertain to what John of the Cross deems to be the sensitive part of our soul. We also have what he calls the spiritual part, which the Carmelite Master, following St. Augustine, identifies as our intellect, will and memory – our capacities to contemplate the truth, to love the good and to be self-aware of our love and knowledge.

The night of the senses involves primarily the sensitive part of our being and the exterior manner of life pertaining to these powers. The outer shell of our existence must be submitted to Christ if we are to become stable in our spiritual life. Those who pass through this night of the senses discover a peace the world cannot give.

Once we have matured, we can also experience a deeper night, the night of the spirit. This difficult purification concerns primarily the spiritual part of our being. If these trials are like a crucifixion, it is because these souls are becoming like St. Paul – perfect imitators of Christ. Filled with love to the brim, they are able to suffer all things through Him who strengthens them. They are also a source of living waters for others because they reveal the joy of heaven even in the midst of the sorrows of earth.

Whatever night we are suffering, because of the unity of our being, our whole being suffers the darkness. Nothing makes sense. At the same time, all of one's weaknesses and inadequacies seem exposed. The soul feels very insecure and needy. What the Lord does to purify our emotional sensitivity in the Night of the Senses is analogous to what He accomplishes in spiritual receptivity in the Night of the Spirit.[49]

---

[48] See *Ascent to Mt. Carmel*, 1.2-3

[49] St. John of the Cross treats the Night of the Senses in *Ascent to Mount Carmel*, book 1 and in *Dark Night of the Soul*, book 1. He treats the Night of the

Not only are the experiences we suffer in the nights analogous, but they are also both related to purification of sin and its effects of sin. In both nights, natural capacities are animated by supernatural life. Appropriate to what the Lord is mysteriously accomplishing in these vital moments of spiritual growth, both nights also realize whole new depths of union with God.

In so far as sin and its effects are being purged and healed, the night is like a fire burning in the soul. Among the effects of sin is ignorance, and in this experience of grace, our dehumanizing ignorance of the ways of God is exposed. What we thought was normal because we were so accustomed to our misery we suddenly discover is not normal at all.

The truth is that God is not destroying our natural capacity to understand or determine the truth. Instead, He is but supernaturally expanding it so that we become capable of discerning His loving will in a more profound way. He is providing a new standard of judgment that ultimately purifies, strengthens and lifts high our natural reasoning powers so that we are no longer driven or even influenced by irrational impulses.

There is one more decisive characteristic shared in the night of the senses and of the spirit, one that we have pointed out before as a paradox but one we cannot emphasize enough: in each night, even though it feels like God is absent, He is really more present than He ever has been before. He is so unfamiliar to us that when He discloses Himself to us in a new way we do not recognize Him at first. We feel like He is not there only because who He is and what we think He is are so dissimilar.

This is like the experience of the disciples on the road to Emmaus. He accompanies us even as we are overcome with sorrow over the tragic disappointments of our lives. Only after this

---

Spirit in *Ascent to Mount Carmel*, book 2 and 3 and in *Dark Night of the Soul*, book 2. He constantly refers back to the major themes of these teachings throughout his works in both his commentaries and his poetry so that imagery from one poem illumines the commentary on another and vice versa.

encounter do we realize our hearts were burning while He walked with us on the way.

In this context, it is also important to emphasize that the suffering is intense because of the immeasurable proportions of God's love for us. The intensity of our thirst for Him is something He produces in us. This immeasurable thirst for God in his felt absence is commensurate with the unimaginable immensity of the glory He longs for us to know.[50]

The nights through which we pass in our pilgrimage of prayer require determined effort on our part as well as vulnerability to God's work in us. This difference between our work and God's work is what St. John of the Cross distinguishes as the active and passive phases of the night. These phases play out in both the night of the senses and the night of the spirit. Each night requires that we live a disciplined life and but even more, each also requires that we welcome all the new mysterious ways the Lord works in us.[51]

As we go on to discuss the active and passive phases of the night, it is important to note that they are not successive in a mechanical way. Instead, God's work and our response to Him flow into each other as part of a beautiful grace. It is like a dance. God's action and our response in faith go hand in hand.

The Active Night

We will now proceed to consider more precisely St. John of the Cross's counsel regarding the spiritual activity that we are supposed to take up. He recommends what we have discussed in terms of *conversatio morum*, an ongoing examination of one's life in the light of the life of Christ. So we must study the life of Christ

---

[50] See *Living Flame of Love*, stanza 3, 22.
[51] The active dimension for both the night of the senses and the night of the spirit is elucidated in *Ascent to Mount Carmel* while the passive phase for these nights is discussed in *Dark Night of the Soul*.

and ponder his radical obedience and devotion to the Father. He is convinced that if we do this, we will see that Jesus never did anything except for the glory of God. Likewise, we must imitate Christ and renounce everything that is not purely for the glory of God in our lives.[52]

This does not mean never doing anything fun or relaxing. God created a beautiful world for us and it gives Him glory when we enjoy this wonderful gift He has entrusted to our care. St. John of the Cross loved to go on hikes and camping trips. Blessed John Paul II loved to go skiing. Blessed Pier Giorgio Frassati loved to climb mountains. These saints help us see that the glory of God is man fully alive.

At the same time, all forms of indulgent behavior, insobriety and anxiety over the things of this world must be renounced. None of this glorifies God. Those driven by pleasure or trying to escape suffering or grasping for control—they are not really living; they are barely existing.

God works through the world He has put us in. If we are unable to engage reality because we have wasted our energy on activities beneath our dignity, we will not have all the resources we need to respond to His invitation. To be vulnerable to what God desires to accomplish, we need to engage realities of life unencumbered by anything unworthy of our humanity.

True freedom by which we thrive is not reducible to the ability to pursue selfish whims. We all have tendencies, as well as the freedom, to choose the merely comfortable or the purely intoxicating. All the same, it is beneath the dignity of the human person to be principally driven by love for anything other than God Himself and, though only secondarily, for those whom God has given us to love for His glory. It is on this point that St. John of the Cross recommends that we act against these tendencies so that instead of being driven by anything that is not God, we might virtuously live lives of real freedom – the freedom to love.

---

[52] For this discussion, see *Ascent to Mount Carmel*, book 1, chapter 13.

God loves our human freedom even more than we do and only in Him does it realize its full potential for love. In fact, God is the source of even greater kinds of liberty if we entrust our freedom to Him. He understands how our freedom is ordered to love and gently prompts it to this end when we make Him the priority of our hearts.

This is where the Carmelite Master's famous doctrine of *Nada* takes it proper place. In any given situation we can choose what is easier or what is more difficult, what is comfortable or what is not comfortable, what is pleasant or what is not pleasant, what everyone holds in great esteem or what is not esteemed by anyone. St. John of the Cross recommends that we train ourselves for spiritual freedom by acting against our tendency to choose what is easy, comfortable, pleasant or popular. This does not mean that such things are bad in themselves. It is just that as long as our desires for them are driving us, we are not really free to live for the glory of God.

Behind his teaching is the truth that love requires the ability to make sacrifices, and love of God is no different. If we are so addicted to what is comfortable that we cannot deny ourselves a little so that someone else might have the food, clothes, shelter or simply the company they need, we are trapped in the misery of a half-lived humanity. The heart that disciplines itself, that puts to death irrational desires, may for a time feel as if it has been deprived. This is the same heart however that is acquiring the inner freedom that will allow the Lord to raise it on high.

The Little Way and the Night

St. Therese of Lisieux develops a compelling application of the doctrine of St. John of the Cross with what she calls her "Little

95

Way."[53] Before her early entrance into Carmel, St. Therese rode an elevator during a pilgrimage to Rome.   The invention was brand new and made her think that Christians needed a new spiritual invention to make it easier to ascend to heaven.

Heroic feats of physical asceticism widely practiced in her day are not sustainable for most Catholics, and yet at the same time, they are sometimes presumed to be the only real path to sanctity. Thérèse Martin felt herself incapable of such feats.   Accordingly, she decided to ask Jesus to be her holiness in all the little things of life.

The *Little Way* is to live by love for Christ in all things. She could do this because she believed it was really His love in her. Every time there was an opportunity to do something that needed to be done but no one else wanted to do it, she would.

The Little Way also requires renunciation. If she could not say something with love, she would not say it.   When she was falsely accused, rather than defending herself, she chose to silently accept the injustice. On the other hand, she would admonish sycophants even though she risked the misunderstanding of her superiors.

These are small ways of acting against the tendency to want to be liked and favored.   By acting against them, she knew she was making space for the holiness of the Lord in her heart. In fact, she believed that she could not even do these "small" acts of love unless He himself provided this love for her.

How did she discover this "Little Way" and what was her secret? She relates in her *Story of a Soul* that her spiritual life really began on Christmas Eve.[54]   After Midnight Mass, her father had the custom of distributing gifts.

---

[53] See *Story of a Soul: Autobiography of St. Therese of Lisieux*, translated by John Clarke, O.C.D., Washington D.C.: ICS Publications (1975, 1976, 3rd ed. 1996) 270ff.
[54] See *Story of a Soul*, 95ff.

In 1886, fourteen-year-old Marie-Françoise-Thérèse was not so little anymore. Her father exclaimed out loud that he was looking forward to no longer having to carry out this particular family ritual. He did not know that his comment, said out of irritation and fatigue, cut his youngest daughter straight to the heart.

Emotionally sensitive and needy especially after the death of her mother some years before, Thérèse stormed upstairs ready explode into tears. Her sisters had seen it all before and braced for a tantrum. What they expected, to their surprise, never came.

Instead, Thérèse suddenly stopped, turned around and went back down to her father. She was actually bubbling with joy and affection as if nothing had ever bothered her at all. That Christmas was remembered with special fondness. The future doctor of the church had received a remarkable moment of grace, one she considered to be her total conversion.

The truth about such moments of grace is that God always provides just what we need. At the same time, He also respects our free will. Thus, He never imposes His grace on us, but rather quietly invites us. It was precisely this kind of moment Thérèse had before her at the top of that staircase.

Grace was being offered for her to act in full freedom, even against her emotional sensitivity. In her heart, in a moment of deep prayer hidden from everyone but herself and the Lord, she said "yes" to his grace and "no" to her temper. A new self-control flooded her heart. She chose to make that Christmas Eve about her whole family having the joy of the Lord, and she chose to do this out of love for Jesus. When St. John of the Cross counsels austere practices he says will help us enter into the dark night, it is precisely this kind of grace he is hoping we will discover.

The Passive Night

Those who strive to enter into the Dark Night and embark upon this Little Way begin to know the victory of Christ over the power of sin. However, this pathway is counter intuitive, even paradoxical. Initially, religion and spirituality become easier and more enjoyable because the virtuous life without the burden of guilt is simply a more pleasant way to live. Then, whether it happens suddenly or gradually, intensely or imperceptibly, this initial enthusiasm disappears.

It is when the enthusiasm disappears that the passive phase of the dark night begins. While maintaining our discipline of life, we also need to welcome a new work that God undertakes in the soul. Night descends on our spiritual life when one begins to wonder whether the intimacy once enjoyed with the Lord in prayer was ever real.

Though it is not the case, we cannot help but think that our weaknesses have so disappointed God; He has abandoned us. Prayer becomes a chore and a certain spiritual weariness takes hold. It is nearly impossible to concentrate or remain recollected in these periods of difficult trial.

St. Teresa of Avila, before her conversion, gave up the practice of prayer at precisely this point. Prayer did not make sense for her, so she let it go even though her conscience invited her to do differently. She had devotion, even though prayer was distasteful to her. She just chose not to use it.

Paradoxically, if we forsake not the discipline of love including the practice of frequent confession, this discouragement is evidence that God is at work. His work is hidden and because we do not understand it, it is like trying to walk in the middle of the night. Although we cannot concentrate, we are drawn into a deep silence, a spiritual place where God has the freedom to accomplish new wonders in us and through us.

This deep silence is no empty void. God fills it with a fullness of meaning, a meaning that can only be understood if we abandon ourselves to Him in faith. Often what God is bringing to surface in our journey is something that was always there but that we were not ready to face. Namely, this is our lack of faith, our lack of confidence, in God. God is working in a very beautiful way to begin to address this poverty.

The Carmelite Masters indicate that our desire to remain silent in this spiritual darkness is not an obstacle on our pilgrimage of faith, but instead they insist it is a precious grace to be greatly desired. It is in this darkness that our journey to the Bridegroom becomes especially tender, a real heart to heart. And we do not even realize it. Carmelites suggest that when God lulls our own psychological powers into this kind of spiritual sleep, in the substance of our soul we discover the interior liberty to surrender to the beauty He discloses to us.

St. John of the Cross's doctrinal vision helps to guide us through this night. According to him, these kinds of graces in prayer are part of the "passive purgation" of either the sensitive or spiritual dimensions of the human person. Presuming we are living lives converted to the Lord, he recommends that we persevere in the silent prayer to which we are drawn.

No technique or method is really helpful and, frankly, the one suffering such difficulties is not inclined to try to do anything at all. Such a soul feels the need to sit silently with the Lord and attend to His presence in the heart even though nothing is sensed or intuited. The Carmelite Master calls such a posture in prayer spiritual nakedness, an image of total vulnerability and trust before the Lord.

God is taking out debris from the great caverns of our soul, debris we could never remove on our own. While he undertakes this work, we suffer a difficult emptiness. The suffering gets more intense until He comes to fill us with the ocean of His love.

He is present to us in a new way, and this new presence is so bright and powerful that our natural powers are temporarily blinded and unable to perceive his glory. We are also suffering the truth about ourselves. We have limits with which the Lord fashioned us. We see imperfection and He sees His power at work in us. These limits are precisely where the Lord wants to touch us with his limitedness.

There is pettiness, mean-spiritedness, greed, and arrogance in us about spiritual things. Often we do not will such movements of the heart, and they are easier to renounce when the object is not spiritual. How can God heal these broken impulses that impede our freedom? How can He transform them into rivers of grace?

Part of being spiritually healed is becoming aware of the actual misery we are in. The Lord gives us this awareness for only one reason: that we might trust Him more completely. He does not want us to rely on what feels good or what we can figure out by clever calculation. He wants us to rely on Him by *love-filled* faith alone.

As we learn this in the difficult school of spiritual suffering, the same impulses that once inclined us to sin now incline us to beg for mercy, to realize how much we need Him. This is the beginning of a great transformation. The power of God is forming our voids and inadequacies so that they might manifest His glory.

The doctrine of persevering in silent prayer throughout the dark night is deeply rooted in two Scriptural truths. The most important truth is that Jesus is always faithful (2 Tim. 2:11-13). He promised that even though the heavens and the earth pass away, his word would never pass away (Mk 13:31).[55] We can have total confidence in Him, always.

The second truth is that the deepest and most powerful experiences of prayer always involve our weaknesses, because St. Paul explains, it is in our weakness that His power is brought to perfection (2 Cor. 12:9). In other words, those who suffer these

---

[55] Pope Benedict points out, "This personalistic focus, this transformation of the apocalyptic visions – which still corresponds to the inner meaning of the Old Testament images --- is the original element in Jesus' teaching about the end of the world: this is what it is all about." *Jesus of Nazareth, Part Two: Holy Week From the Entrance Into Jerusalem to the Resurrection*, Trans. Philip J. Whitmore, San Francisco: Ignatius Press (2011) 51.

difficult nights in their pilgrimage of prayer know, like no one else ever will, the faithfulness and the power of God.

St. John of the Cross's *Dark Night* allows us to hear the voice of someone who came to love what God does in these difficult trials of prayer. With language that evokes his own escape from prison, this doctor of prayer describes a lover, inflamed with love, sneaking out of her house in disguise while it is all dark and no one knows what she is doing. She is on a quest and has patiently waited for this lucky moment. Now, she can go out and find the one for whom her heart longs with no one to distract or detain her any longer.

There is a story about Mother Teresa trying to comfort a very sick and dying woman. She was in great pain both physically and emotionally. At the same time, her faith was beautiful. In the midst of horrific misfortune, she was receiving sheer grace, in the form of a disguised but deep spiritual joy that overflowed to everyone. Mother Teresa told her that this suffering was a kiss from Jesus. She smiled at Mother Teresa, folded her hands, and said, "Please tell Jesus to stop kissing me."[56]

---

[56] Teresa of Calcutta, *Love: A Fruit Always in Season, Daily Meditations*, ed. Dorothy S. Hunt, San Francisco: Ignatius Press (1987) 91-92.

Chapter Six
Prayer as Spiritual Combat

"Peace depends on victory, and victory depends on struggle. If you desire peace, you will struggle continuously.

"Your 'weapons' in this struggle are meditation, self-denial, the sacraments, the rosary, and recollection. Your allies are Mary, Joseph, the angels, your patron saints, and your spiritual director. Unless you gradually drop your weapons or betray your allies, your victory is assured."[57]

After God awakens us spiritually and we set out on a pilgrimage through the darkness of our hearts to find Him, we soon discover that this quest is being taken up in the midst of a great spiritual war. Unlike a platonic worldview where the higher realms of spiritual existence are more peaceful than the lower worlds of material being, our apostolic faith reveals there is war in heaven, and the earth is an enemy-occupied battlefield.[58] The enemies we confront in this war and the battles we are given to fight are not distractions. God uses these spiritual enemies who stand in our way to lead us deeper into the mysterious nights in which He awaits us in love.

The battle for the heart is waged in the mind, or so the Desert Fathers taught. Seeking the truth about God is the only way

---

[57] Francis Xavier Cardinal Nguyen Van Thuan, *The Road to Hope: A Gospel from Prison*, Trans. Peter Bookallil, Boston: Pauline Books and Media (2001) 17.

[58] See for example Revelation 12:7-12 and Ephesians 6:11-18. St. Athanasius presents the ascetic as a champion in this battle, see his *Life of Antony*.

to realize the victory He won for us. Although the victory of good over evil is already won, this victory can only be realized on a personal level in each individual heart through the grace of God. The decision of the heart to cling to God requires a loving knowledge of the truth. As long as we allow our lives to be guided by fantasy or inordinate desires, the heart is robbed of the truth it needs to choose good and avoid evil.

Sometimes we do not pray because the truth of prayer has been obscured. In a culture in which value is assigned either by productivity or entertainment, prayer appears out of place. True prayer is nonetheless neither an inefficient use of time nor an entertaining diversion from what is really important. We fight for the truth by prayer so that we might live by the truth in our hearts.

We need prayer, not because of anything it produces, but because we need God. When prayer is rooted in truth, it opens us to this beautiful knowledge of the heart, a loving knowledge that fills life with meaning and harmony. For when doctrine and prayer converge in an encounter with Christ, the music of heaven echoes on earth.

Seeking the Truth in Prayer

How do we know whether our prayer is rational, a true encounter with the Lord? Prayer is "rational" when it is "in right relation to" and "in harmony with" with reality. Prayer bears an intelligent relation with what truly is. It stands up humanity on the very ground of all existence and knowledge: God Himself. Here, human reason raised in prayer dances with Eternal Truth. Jesus is this Truth. All that God has wanted to reveal about Himself is revealed in Christ. That is why the Gospel of John reveals Him as the Word of the Father.

Truth protects prayer from self-deception. My own contemplation, after all, can be an escape into fantasy, a sham indulged in to divert attention from the overwhelming misery gripping my heart. Even my good works for others can sometimes be little more than an expression of my need to have others think well of me. This is why Jesus taught that not everyone who calls out "Lord, Lord" would inherit the Kingdom of God.

In the spiritual life, the truth revealed by God is not only our escape from the overbearing ego that imprisons us; it is also a powerful weapon for human dignity. This truth is what the Church communicates through sacred doctrine. When prayer is imbued with this truth, it becomes a channel through which the Lord confronts the irrationality choking out all that is good and noble in humanity.

Prayer rooted in the truth makes space in human life for God to act. It provides the required silence for the harmony of Divine Glory to ring forth. It brings us into a beautiful night where Christ the radiant star can captivate us and lead us on our way.

In order to clarify this, it might be helpful to refer St. Thomas Aquinas doctrine: *oratio dicitur quasi oris ratio*.[59] He is basically saying that prayer "*oratio*" is a mouthful of reason "*oris ratio*" (literally, reason of the mouth). Faith, in fact, opens our hearts to an intelligent conversation with God, a conversation in which the truth matters. Such a conversation, to be a real conversation, means a sharing of the minds. The person who prays is meant to participate in the very mind of God.

While many look at prayer as an impulse of will towards God, prayer is more than the heart intending something. Although it is true that holy desires move us to pray, prayer itself extends beyond desire and engages all the powers of our soul. [60] In this way, prayer is the highest and noblest of all human activities: a total engagement of the highest functions of our intelligence to

---

[59] "Prayer is like reason from the mouth," *Summa Theologica* II-II, q.83 a.1.
[60] See St. Augustine, Letter 130, *Letter to Proba*.

their fullest potential on the most important, most vital matters of existence.

In God's eyes, one human thought, filled with faith, is worth more than the whole tangible world.[61] Because of the unique place of humanity in the center of the visible cosmos, the prayer of faith establishes true order – from the most interior realities of the heart to the concrete physical circumstances of the world in which we dwell.   This is because prayer is in a special way an act of *grace permeated reason,* humble human thought raised up into the mind of God by the Word of the Father bringing order to all of creation.

Is Christian prayer really this powerful? Does it really claim to have a role in the transformation of the whole cosmos? A word, any word, can be a powerful thing if said in the right way, at the right time, to the right person and for the right reason. This is because a word, even in frail human speech, mediates truth; it has the power to convey the truth with love. Christ has taken up this power sewn into human nature and offered it to the glory of the Father. With Him, Christian prayer can do anything.

The Word of the Father fills us with the words of prayer, even when human speech fails to articulate what He discloses in our spirit.   At the same time, the intelligibility and purpose of all creation flows from and leads to this Divine Word who became flesh. Christian prayer is rooted in this reality, the reality of the Word. When we gaze into the eyes of Christ with the eyes of our heart, we begin to see things as they truly are. Under His gaze of love, our prayer is made to resonate with the will of the Father.

The Greatness of Christian Prayer
in the Battle for Humanity

The Apostle Paul exclaims that the mystery of Christian piety is great. The discipline of the Lord entails a filial piety that

---

[61] See St. John of the Cross, *Sayings of Light and Love,* #35.

begins and ends with prayer. Christ's confident and humble cry to the Father reveals His deepest desires and only those who enter into His prayer really come to understand his heart.

In Christian piety, the mystery of devotion, and our efforts at beginning to pray are about entering ever more deeply into the heart of Christ. From his heart, an endless sea of the deepest desires flow, desires that resonate with the will of the Father. The most intimate of these was offered the night before he died, *"Father, I will that where I am, those whom you have given me may be there with me so that they might contemplate the glory you have given me from before the creation of the world" (Jn. 17:24).*[62]

This prayer of Jesus, uttered with full knowledge of His impending passion and death, assumes we understand what glory the Father gave and continues to give to Jesus. Glory is the radiance of personal greatness, and true glory is almost always hidden in this world. The one who sees someone in his glory really knows the truth about that person. To see the glory of the Lord is to know who He is.

We come again to the great truth: the glory of God is man fully alive and the life of man is the vision of God. This means men and women live life to the full when they take time to gaze on the Word of God in faith. Human life is lived to the full when it is fully given to God and to those God entrusts to us. This has to do with the Holy Trinity in Whose image we are made. Like the Father, Son and Holy Spirit, we are made to be in a loving communion. The blood of Christ has given us access to this mystery. If we contemplate this loving communion in faith we not only see a pattern for how we ought to live, but we receive the power to live in the likeness of God.

Jesus longs for His disciples to have an abundantly fulfilling life. Not simply happy within the bounds of this present life, but extremely so in ways that this present life cannot contain. When men and women thrive to the full, they give God glory be-

---

[62] St. Paul sheds light on this prayer of Jesus in 2 Cor. 3:18.

cause they are in His image: when they are happy, they are more like Him. The more like Him they are, the more they reveal His glory.

Jesus made this kind of life possible when He died on the Cross. Because of sin, we were cut off from this fullness of life. Before Christ, the miserable absence of love in our hearts blinded and weakened us so that we could not attain our true good. Our own hostility constantly threatened our very existence. The Lord could not watch indifferently when the noble goodness with which He endowed us was subject to such futility. He set out to save us.

Since He is the Word of the Father, whatever He enters into receives purpose and meaning. When He entered into fallen humanity, He brought our nature into harmony with God's will to raise us up. Yet this was done at a great price.

To reveal to us the greatness of God's love, Jesus entered into the terrible mystery of our suffering. One only truly enters the heart of another when one embraces the suffering that is there. When the Eternal Word emptied Himself of heavenly glory and took on the humility of our condition, He embraced our suffering all the way to the Cross.

Catherine of Siena offers a great insight along these lines: the Cross is the Lord's bridge into the heart of man and man's bridge into the Heart of God. By crossing this bridge, God has given reason and purpose to human life. Through the encounter of the Crucified God dwelling in one's own heart, each discovers that there is *Someone* who loves him. When anyone accepts this love, such a person feels compelled to pick up his own cross and follow the God-Man into the hearts of those to whom he is led.

Such a life is ordered to a new kind of society, an authentic communion and friendship with God and with one another. Whenever this new life begins again, Jesus' prayer "that they may be one" is realized. The glory of the Cross is revealed.

The world is being ordered for a new kind of society, and this society is being realized all the time. The Risen Lord is in communion with the Father, in a forever new society of profound joy and love, a fellowship entered into not only at the end of life, but right now in prayer. Prayer allows this society to break into this world, establishing a culture of life and giving birth to a civilization of love.

Prayer, because it makes space for God to order the world so that humanity might thrive to the full, is thus, fundamentally, an act of grace-imbued intelligence. Once we understand that prayer involves supernatural rationality, the nature of things opposed to prayer becomes clear. All forms of irrationality stand as the adversaries to prayer. Prayer grows in freedom and truth the more it confronts and overcomes irrationality. Yet the forms of irrationality are more vast, ancient and clever than human intelligence can cope with alone. In order for prayer to mature, it must take up a spiritual battle against these forces, and it must do so wrapped in faith and completely reliant on God.

The Enemies of Prayer

The Christian tradition knows three principle enemies of prayer: the world, the flesh and the devil. St. John of the Cross describes these as wild animals, frontiers and thugs.[63] In order to progress on our journey into intimacy with Christ we must confront the world, all kinds of irrational powers and even our own hostility to the Lord.

On Facing the Wild Beasts

---

[63] See his commentary *Spiritual Canticle*, 3. 1-10. *Thugs* may not precisely translate the term used by the Carmelite Master. However, translating *los fuertes* as merely *strong men* sounds too benign for the trouble irrational forces cause the spiritual life. Ruffians, brutes or bullies would be closer to what he describes. This text will refer to *los fuertes* as *thugs*.

Like a wild beast the world attempts to frighten genuinely spiritual people. It sees the spiritual freedom they have in Christ frightening. This was true in the Christian world of St. John of the Cross where worldly people who had authority in the Church imprisoned and tortured him. It is even truer today in the culture of death that has taken hold.

In a culture of death, worldly powers find it inconvenient to be reminded of the heartless brutality perpetrated against the most vulnerable in our society. Those who are enslaved to their reputation, comfort, and security often aid these financial, cultural and political powers. If we are afraid to be inconvenienced by the good and beautiful in life—like the unborn or the elderly—we are easily manipulated into pretending that indifference is not that bad.

On the other hand, if someone is not motivated by these worldly values, the world perceives such a person as a risk to the *status quo*. Like wild animals, the culturally, politically and financially powerful intimidate by making an aggressive display of social hostility. Today, Christians are all too often shamed into silence in the arena of public opinion while the noisy bigotry against the Church has grown fierce: a virtual *Circus Maximus*. It is in fact the case that the ancient social hostility towards the Christian faith is no anachronism of the distant past. To this end, the entertainment industrial complex in America has been unrestrained in portraying dedicated people of faith as bogeymen: ignorant, hypocritical, dowdy, villainous.

Should anyone dare to speak out for Christian moral principles and religious institutions, they should be ready also to be mocked before crowds conditioned to gleefully applaud the lack of civility. Freedom to express one's love for God through public works is now diminished by historical proportions in the United States and around the world. At the same time, primordial institutions that have always protected what is most beautiful about humanity, like marriage and family, are vulnerable to the whims of legislators and judiciaries. This climate, however, makes it easier to confront the world with its own prejudice. Here, a life of prayer provides courage to stand firm.

Once a reporter challenged Archbishop Charles Chaput, O.F.M.Cap., who at the time was the Archbishop of Denver. The reporter asked him why he was forcing his values on society. The Archbishop quipped back that if he did not impose his values the media would impose its own values. And, he continued, his values are better than those of the media. Rather than allow the reporter to define his role, the Archbishop turned the table and challenged the reporter to think about his own role and his own values.

This exchange shows that, against any religious prejudice which tries to shame Christians into silence, the power of confidently speaking the truth in love is invincible. Christians do not admit of being merely passive spectators in life. They are at the center of the drama that plays out and society needs their witness. As Blessed John Paul II declared in Denver, we must be proud to proclaim the gospel of Christ from the rooftops.

Before the world can be confronted in the marketplace of ideas, we need to confront its suggestions that have taken root in our hearts. Frequent confession and prayerful examination of one's life is very helpful. We must constantly examine whether our use of entertainment and technology is really giving glory to God. Also helpful is a certain amount of asceticism and sobriety when it comes to using the media. While awareness of what is going on in the world helps us to engage the fray, mental prayer is a better preparation than merely consuming the news cycle.

Against the world's hostility to the truth about God and humanity, authentic Christianity has always been subversive just as was Christ Himself during his earthly ministry. St. John of the Cross explains that we must deal with social forces the same way one would deal with a wild beast. We must not be afraid nor retreat into cowardice. Instead, we must hold fast to the truth, live

110

it out and boldly proclaim it. The world is the easiest of the enemies of prayer to overcome: it cannot stand up to the truth.

Crossing the Frontiers of our Humanity

Our flesh also tries to limit our devotion to the Lord. We can get bored with holy things and become discouraged in prayer because psychologically we resist change. Yet this does not get to the sense in which St. John of the Cross understands our flesh as a frontier. He viewed the frontier as a dangerous, untamed place, through which we must pass so that we could come into the safety of a deeper union with God.

This suggests that we are limited until we are led beyond our own sinful propensities. If we do not go beyond our sinfulness, if we do not fight our propensity to be self-indulgent or our desire to escape life through insobriety, we will never find the One for whom we yearn. Yet the Bridegroom, precisely because He loves us, leads us through all the ways we have limited ourselves. It is our devotion to Christ and even more, His devotion to us, that gets us through these frontiers.

St. John of the Cross is tapping into a great theme of western spirituality. As a people, we understand ourselves as *homo viator* – pilgrims or refugees, displaced and wandering on a quest for our true home. Along these lines, Virgil's Aeneas and Dante's pilgrim are sent on quests guided by divine power. This resonates with Abraham's pilgrimage of faith.

Aeneas escapes the burning vestiges of Troy to become a forefather of Rome, the whole time tested by the gods. The pilgrim Dante, exiled from Florence, must find his way out of a mid-life crisis by journeying through hell-fire to the beatific vision led forth by poetry, human love and sanctity. Abraham sets out from the Land of Ur in humble trust under the guiding hand of God, himself tested time and again until he takes on the very likeness of the mysterious Presence who chose him.

The stories of our culture and the revelation of our faith indicate that we must go on a journey against the natural flow of events. We are not meant to perish with Troy or be eaten by beasts in the dark forests of Italy. We cannot remain in the comfortable ways of our forefathers in Ur. We are to set out, move beyond the status quo, and exert the effort it takes to follow God. He leads us beyond the boundaries and limits of our ability to love Him and one another. To be successful in our own quest, we must let go of dreams that are holding us back and open ourselves up to the new horizons of God.

The Frontiers St. Teresa of Avila Crossed

Teresa of Avila contended with this reality. Even after her conversion and her renewed dedication to prayer, she was still attached to certain friendships that were not spiritually uplifting. As long as relationships are ordered to the glory of God, there really is not a problem. The problem comes when we hang on to certain relationships out of sentimentalty or because we want to impress others or because we have something to gain by them.

If we are really honest, we know that such inordinate attachments are holding us back or even pulling us down. When such relationships hamper our life of prayer, it is important that we renounce them. Otherwise, emotional energy and attention that belongs to God, and those God has entrusted to us, is dissipated on pursuits not worthy of our dignity. It is precisely this that Teresa of Avila recognized she must do, but she had no idea how to do it.

A great saint, St. Francis Borgia, S.J., actually helped her move past this frontier in her life. A Spanish nobleman, theologian and widower, Francis gave up his duchy and royal title to become a Jesuit. He was noted not only for his considerable administrative ability but also for his life of contemplation and gifts as a great spiritual director.

Saint Teresa poured out her soul to him including the particular problem she was having with sinful attachments and unhealthy relationships. While there was nothing immoral about the friendships, they were not helping her pray and she needed to cross this frontier if she was to enter into deeper friendship with the Lord. Whereas other spiritual directors were inclined to simply admonish her lack of maturity and direct her to more austere ascetical practices, this contemplative Jesuit carefully discerned the remarkable ways the Lord was present in her life of prayer. He noted how thinking about His passion made her vulnerable to what Christ wanted to accomplish in her. Although she was led to believe that she ought to go beyond her imagination, the saint told her that she needed to begin her prayer by thinking about Christ crucified. He also encouraged her not to resist the graces that the Lord wanted to pour out on her, but instead to allow the Lord to take her spiritually wherever He desired. Similarly another Jesuit confessor told her to take the whole matter to prayer by singing the *Veni Creator Spiritus*.

As she sang this beautiful invocation to the Holy Spirit, her heart was lifted up to the Lord in an ecstatic prayer she calls "rapture." Caught up in the love of God, she felt herself freed from the need to be loved by those who were dragging her down. The point is, in order to pass beyond the weaknesses of our frail humanity, it is not always enough to make a good resolution and then act on it. Sometimes, in difficult renunciations, we must go deeper into prayer and allow the Lord to lift us up with His own hands.

Confronting Oppressive Irrational Forces

Besides the world and the flesh, there are also super-intelligent irrational powers that are bent on our destruction. Their freedom to harm us is severely limited, as long as we hold fast to Christ. Nonetheless, for reasons known to Him alone, the

Lord sometimes allows these creatures to test us. These trials can help break us of our tendency to be self-reliant and not to trust in power of God.

In other words, spiritual battles against powers of oppressive irrationality help us mature spiritually. When we resist and overcome every form of irrationality, we discover deeper and more wonderful ways of relying on Christ Jesus. He is the Truth that exposes and triumphs over every threat to our dignity.

Christ crucified is our Deliverer when we must deal with the Satan whose name means "adversary." He is also called "the accuser" because he constantly condemns us before God and one another. Utterly devoid of love of God, his cunning malice towards us is driven by envy.

Whereas the world might try to frighten us with loud noise and empty threats, the thugs who serve this adversary can sometimes hurt us like a thorn in the flesh. They confuse with all kinds of clever snares. They plant such gloomy thoughts it seems as if one's whole life has gone amiss. They also humiliate in efforts to make us completely lose heart. We cannot resist such demoralizing oppression on our own.

St. John of the Cross explains, however, such forces cannot stand against the Lord. The Living God delivers us when we humble ourselves and seek help. Through the Church, He reveals the victory of good over evil—for the power of God is made perfect in our weakness.[64]

These enemies – the world, the flesh and the devil – do not usually come at us one at a time in obvious ways. They are joined together in an unholy alliance. The gift of discernment is needed so that we know when the Lord is helping us cross the frontiers of our humanity, when we need to stand firm against the angry threats of the world, and when we need to seek help in dealing with spiritual thugs. In the heat of the moment, such discernment comes whenever it is needed for those who maintain the disci-

---

[64] See 2 Corinthians 12:7-9.

pline of prayer. Indeed, for the prayerful, victory in this spiritual battle is assured.

Anachoresis – victory through retreat

If the spiritual battle fought in prayer requires discernment, discernment requires stepping back. When we step back from a situation we are often able to see what is really going on even on a natural level. Similarly, if prayer involves spiritual battle, the way we emerge victorious is paradoxical: it is by retreat.

This specific retreat involves a pilgrimage away from superficial reactions in the moment and into the desires of the Lord's heart. The ancient mystics of the Church called this journey into silence *withdrawal*. An *anchorite* is someone who *withdraws* from the world and into his heart.

The modern idea of *going on retreat* is aimed at the same movement. The need to withdraw from worldly affairs is experienced again and again in the Church. Some look at this as escapism, a running away from difficult issues. But those who allow the Lord to lead them into His silence soon discover that they are not running away at all. Instead, through withdrawing from superficial distractions; they find themselves in a place where they can finally deal with the real problems of life.

Entering into silence is essential to prayer and a part of this pilgrimage to the Lord to which contemplatives bear witness. Prayer requires a readiness to give up being in control or the center of attention. We must do this in order to attend to the Lord and surrender to His love. It is natural to want to be known and loved by others, to be the center of attention, to be in control. But if this desire is not given to the Lord, if it is what dominates our lives, we become slaves to our own ego. We are self-pre-occupied.

Self-pre-occupation is an interior noise that distracts from the Lord, and then distracted we are not free to hear the Lord whispering His secrets to our hearts. God can help us through

115

this frontier of our humanity but this will require that we surrender to a deeper work of prayer.

To withdraw to be with God disposes us to this deeper work. This kind of prayer pulls us out of ourselves and makes us vulnerable to God. It is not the kind of prayer in which our efforts are as dominant as the Lord's efforts in us. This kind of prayer withdraws us even deeper than we can go on our own. It is called mystical contemplation.

Mystical contemplation is a gift that calls for our surrender. In this prayer in which the Lord withdraws us to Himself, we accept what the Lord is doing and allow Him to do it. Beyond our conscious awareness, the Holy Spirit operates in incomprehensible depths. Such a grace is more powerful than the dynamism of self. While this is true in all prayer, in mystical prayer it is true in an even more profound way. When we sanction the movements of the Holy Spirit in our hearts, we find ourselves pre-occupied something much more wonderful: *Someone* beyond our power to understand.

We will explore how mystical prayer unfolds in chapter 8, our chapter on the secret garden. The point of introducing this kind of prayer is in this discussion of spiritual combat is that fighting for the truth and withdrawing into silence are both deeply connected. God assists us in this struggle when we withdraw and allow Him to draw us. When we surrender to the silent melodies of His love, we recognize the divine harmony that rings through reality and our hearts are filled with that for which we fight. By the confidence this provides, we learn a simple movement of the will, an act of trust that clings to Him—because He is the Truth.

How do we dispose ourselves to this kind of prayer? Renunciation, solitude and silence free the heart to attend to God. This liberation requires time.

The journey of prayer is a pilgrimage not only out of exterior noise but also interior cacophony. Anything that is out of harmony distracts from the still small voice of God whether in the external world around us or in the interior world of our feelings and thoughts. Discouragement, self-pity, righteous indignation, resentment, anxiety over worldly occupations – this is all internal noise. Such noise can drown out the gentle breeze in which the Lord speaks. We must not allow our hearts to be caught up in the currents of such storms.

Storms of Destruction

One thing that is especially dangerous to the solitude required for real prayer is what a psalm describes as "storms of destruction." The context of Psalm 57 is David hiding from Saul in a cave. Saul was given to irrational fits of rage, especially because of his jealousy toward David. David had to flee for his life in the face of Saul's instability: "In the shelter of your wings I take refuge, till the storms of destruction pass by."[65]

The context of Psalm 57 suggests the storm of destruction is not so much a natural disaster as much as it is the violent irrationality of someone close to us. It is so easy to allow irrational aggression to stir up all kinds of hostility in us. This is a trap which, once sprung, robs the soul of the freedom to pray.

Anyone who has struggled not to lash out in anger when irrationally attacked by someone knows that such self-mastery requires special assistance from God. Sometimes there is just no reasoning with someone who is intent on harming us. The humiliating word or the scornful look, when we are unsuspecting, brutally strikes to the core. In the heat of such battles, we do not always know how to be merciful. It seems like anything we try to do in some circumstances will betray God's mercy. So we must withdraw into the "shelter" of God's "wings."

---

[65] *Liturgy of the Hours*, Thursday, Week I, trans. *The Grail*, Collins: London (1963).

Biblically "wings" – whether of eagles, angels or God – are a metaphor for power. Just as a bird soars over the earth, the power of God is over this world including all the events and people He allows into our lives. In the face of all kinds of violence – spiritual, emotional, verbal and also, as in David's case, physical – it is possible to find rest in God. Divine power is the best shield against every form of malice. But we must seek this, and above all trust in Him.

If we are being tested and our weakness is beginning to show, it is only because He desires to show forth his loving power. God's power hides us in the shelter of true solitude and a stronghold of spiritual silence, even in the midst of difficult trials and persecution. How He does this in each set of circumstances is always different. Yet, He never fails to deliver from those storms of destruction anyone who clings to Him.

Withdrawing into solitude, seeking places where time can be spent in silence, is something that we must do, not only physically, but especially spiritually, by begging the Lord for his protection and trusting in his power to establish us in peace. He is the one who makes the kind of peaceful stillness in which a profound encounter with Him can take place. Prayer is less distracted and more focused when both the ears of our body and the ears of our heart are sheltered in His peaceful stillness. Such God-given liberation from noise, especially violent noise, helps prayer mature and become fully human. In the sacred silence of God's own peace, the soul begins to discover the most beautiful and subtle canticles of Divine Love.

The Victory of Good over Evil

Prayer brings us into apocalyptic reality. Each moment of prayer is intimately realized eschatology. We mentioned in our first chapter that prayer involves a moment of judgment. In fact, deep prayer fully anticipates the final judgment. This is why those who go deep into prayer discover heroic levels of courage and deep internal resolve. No matter what unravels around them, they stand on the Word, the Word made Flesh. Just as the Lord preached, "Sun and moon may pass away" but the Word of the Lord, His promise fulfilled in Christ Jesus, "will never fail."[66]

It is in this context that the Lord warns us against self-indulgence, insobriety and anxiety over worldly affairs. These things distract us and dissipate our ability to cling to the Lord when it is most important. Unless we battle to renounce such things, when things fall apart around us, we will not have the strength or desire to pray.

One evening, after taking my son to the hospital, a blood test revealed that John had acute lymphoblastic leukemia. One of the specialists explained that the case was very advanced and that the odds were not in his favor. That night, my world was shaken, and I had to learn to turn to God.

I cannot recall how long I spent kneeling by his bed, but there is a memory of turning my heart to the Lord and entrusting my son to Him. The prayer was punctuated with shock, waves of fear and sorrow, as well as a rush of questions and theories about what had happened. There was also deep compunction over my many failures as a father, and a new realization of just how blessed I was.

Cancer patients and their parents must try to be completely focused during the different regimens of chemotherapy. This was easier for my wife than it was for me. I kept on wanting to know what the whole process would entail. But our doctor insisted on giving only that amount of information we needed for our immediate situation. At each stage, there seemed to be either

---

[66] For a beautiful reflection on this point is on a passage to which referred to earlier in this chapter, see Pope Benedict XVI, *Jesus of Nazareth*, Part 2, *Holy Week: from the Entrance into Jerusalem to the Resurrection*, trans. Philip J. Whitmore, San Francisco: Ignatius Press (2011) 49-52.

some new impossible course of action we had to master or else some horrific procedure my son had to endure.[67]

It was like the spiritual life. We could not do it by ourselves. We had to trust the Lord and the doctor.

Although I am deeply thankful to God and our doctor for the life of my son (both Blessed Elisabeth of the Trinity and Blessed Pier Giorgio Frassati were our special patrons), I recall almost nothing of the whole ordeal, which in fact lasted over a period of years.

Thinking back on that night in the hospital I remain amazed over the presence of God, even though I did not feel it. The pangs of fear, sorrow and regret, even the anger and irritation, the desire to blame something or someone – all of this was a normal, human response to stress. What I still cannot quite understand is that in the face of all the normal human reaction, I also experienced a deep, unshakeable peace.

For those questioning a similar experience, we have had a foretaste of what eternal life and the greatness of our human destiny is all about. This peace, which the Lord provides even in the face of great anxiety, is the fruit of his Uncreated Love at work in us. For me, it seems that for the first time in my life, prayer was not about my own big fat ego. It was not about whether I felt right or felt anything at all. There was no awareness of self at all. My prayer that night was about the Lord and about my son.

For a few moments, sometime in the early morning hours before dawn, I tasted the freedom of real love where no sacrifice, no renunciation, no trial, no temptation is too much for the heart. The Heavens and the Earth could pass away. It would not matter. I was fed by something that endures forever. I know that those who are nourished with this love will never be shaken. They hold

---

[67] For those in the health care professions, it is so important to allow parents to exercise their faith with their children in these moments. Dr. Thomas Smith and his staff were wonderful at this. I would catechize my son on offering things up and pray with him, and sometimes they even joined us.

in their hearts a vision by which they thrive: finally free to be fully human, they are fully alive.

There are those who live in this freedom all the time. They know that the Word of the Lord never passes away and their whole existence is established in Him. These are the citizens of heaven. They know the victory of prayer—and they pray for us that we might know this victory too.

Chapter Seven

Climb the Hidden Mountain

One might consider the Lord's heart a hidden mountain. This spiritual peak is seen only with the eyes of faith. It is also where we feel most at home.

After living a disciplined life for many years, Anthony of the Desert felt called to find this mountain. He sought it at first as a physical place where he might have more solitude. But in prayer, he came to understand that the mountain to which the Lord was calling him was something more than physical.

Finding the hidden mountain is not ever a journey we make on our own. The Lord is always with us. In fact, without Him, we are completely lost. Christ alone can charm, fascinate and draw us to Himself. He seduces us into His great silence.

St. John of the Cross uses the image of Mt. Carmel, the spiritual home of the Carmelite Order. In his teachings, the top of Mt. Carmel is a place of beautiful encounter with the Lord. To get to this place of encounter, one must go by faith.

A path goes up the center of the diagram to the top of the mountain. To the right and to the left he lists all kinds of earthly and spiritual goods and experiences. The diagram indicates that we must go by neither the goods nor experiences of this world; neither must we pursue goods nor experiences of the world to come. Instead, we must pursue the Lord alone. We must serve Him alone.

He means by this that the mountain of prayer cannot be climbed by seeking anything or anyone other than the Lord, and that the only way to find Him is to cleave to Him by living faith. Faith is always directional for him. When one seeks the Lord by faith, the self is never mistaken for God. This is because faith is always ordered to a friendship with the Lord.

Such a relational faith differs from the pursuit of self- satisfying experience; even if it passes through many different kinds of experiences. Nor is faith about acquiring a state of consciousness because it is ordered to a union which goes beyond the boundaries of created consciousness. This faith is radically rooted Word of the Father. It models itself after Christ crucified seeking only that which He sought: to live by love, to do the will of the Father.

A Spiritual Reality in the Real World

Something about mountains inspires prayer and speaks of closeness to God. In the Bible, Christ prays in the mountains as did Moses, Elijah and David. In Southern France, at Sainte Baume, high up against a mountain face right at tree line, there is a grotto where tradition says St. Mary Magdalene lived as an anchorite fasting and praying for the Church. The deep spiritual silence cloaking the place has been noted by great figures like the 19th Century Dominican, Lacordaire and the desert hermit, Charles de Foucauld. Pilgrims still go there today to listen to the Lord. St. Anthony of the Desert also to hear the Lord whisper great secrets into his heart.

Perhaps the most austere of all contemplatives are the Carthusians. High up in the Chartreuse Mountains above Grenoble, France, these men have devoted their lives to listening to God. They do this through living anonymous lives of silence and solitude where the Lord speaks His words of silent love.

In fact, they believe the more anonymous they become, the greater good they do for God. Their monasteries are located in the remote regions of the world. Such contemplative monasteries, even if we never see them, help the whole Church renew its prayer. Indeed, the Grande Chartreuse is a powerful foretaste of heaven and an insight into the human heart.

German film director Philip Gröning produced a beautiful movie called *Into Great Silence* about *La Grande Chartreuse*. The Mother Charterhouse can be cold, windy, austere and, at the same time, stunning. The movie itself conveys the enchanting combination of austerity and joy one finds in withdrawing from the world to be with the Lord. There is hardly any speaking and the only music is the chanting of the monks. The film itself tries to draw the audience into great silence. In one scene, shot from high in the main chapel's loft, looking into the dark abyss below, the camera focuses on the faint glow of a single shining vigil lamp deep in the apse of the sanctuary.

For over eight hundred years, the monks of the Chartreuse Mountains have kept watch, waiting for the coming of the Lord from the middle of the night to the early hours of the morning. As it has been for centuries, their high vaulted chapel, plunged in darkness and bathed in starlight, stands as a place of encounter, a mystical encounter with Christ. Out of these cavernous depths, in both Latin and French, hidden voices began to rise in praise to the Living God, chanting ancient psalms and praying for the salvation of the world.

On the occasion of the Centenary of the life of Blessed Elisabeth of the Trinity, I was given exceptional permission to visit the Grande Chartreuse to make retreat in the guest house and to join in their liturgies. The film cannot quite capture the bone chilling cold one feels while waiting for the mid-night liturgy to begin. Nonetheless, it does capture something of the cavernous abyss which the gothic chapel of the Grand Chartreuse communicates in the darkest hours of the night.

For all the silence enveloping it, fullness fills this chapel. In the light, the stone pours down from heaven while the windows reach for God. At night, in the cavernous pitch black, the same space is all at once a sign of the world and the depths of the heart. On cannot help but think of "the deep caverns of feelings" described by St. John of the Cross.[68] Both the world and the heart are filled with cold dark abysses, but in those harsh places a light promising the presence of Christ shines and heavenly voices of unseen hosts wait in holy vigil.

Just like this chapel, we cannot see into the depths of our own heart and yet all of heaven is there at prayer. This is why prayer must never limit itself to seeking only those experiences of which we can be conscious. Prayer expands into places in our humanity that we cannot perceive, vast spaces that only God understands. He knows us better than we ever will.

God, hidden but present in his very power and glory, constantly stirs a celestial hymn of praise in these mysterious regions of our being. His praise rises up even when we are distracted, or, worse, resisting Him. Even in the face of our rejection, the Lord yearns for us to raise our voices in love to join this secret song of love. For as long as we live, He never loses this hope in us.

This song of the heart is nothing other than the great canticle that we were created to sing: singing it is the source of unimaginable joy, a joy He wants us to know. To join this song, all we need is to be still and listen. As we enter into the Lord, the Great Silence personified, we taste what it means to be fully human and fully alive.

Prayer requires periods where we withdraw from our life activities and turn our attention to the Lord. For those who want a real *conversatio morum*, who yearn for a life *habitare secum*, it is not enough to intend to be open to God if we do not make time in our schedules to attend to His voice. Fasting from noise and rapid succession of images (digital or imaginary), we must make space to listen to the Lord and to gaze on him. As we enter into silence, we begin to see in the vast chamber of the heart the faint glow of a votive candle promising the presence of the Lord; and we experience the resounding echo of heaven's praises being sung within us, and we are invited to share in it.

---

[68] See *Living Flame of Love*, 3:18-23.

The movie *Into Great Silence* discloses the fruits of this encounter with the Lord. Monks are shown at different stages of life: from the springtime of profession to the autumn of the end of life. The camera shows an old blind monk. He witnesses to his ongoing encounter with the Lord that has made him thankful for everything, including his blindness. Through his simple words and charming smile, it is obvious that he sees the world for what it really is and knows the secret to happiness.

To drive this experience home, throughout the film, various scripture verses are projected on the screen. One of these verses is from 1 Kings 19:11-13:

> A mighty hurricane split the mountains and shattered the rocks before the Lord. But the Lord was not in the hurricane. And after the hurricane, an earthquake. But the Lord was not in the earthquake. And after the earthquake, fire. But the Lord was not in the fire. After the fire, a light murmuring sound. And when Elijah heard this, he covered his face and went out.[69]

In silence, something is communicated that is not only informative, but also transformative; and this transformation is not limited to one's own life but extended throughout one's culture and continues to extend into the future. For the saints who practiced this, they became a source of life for others because they drew from the Source of Life Himself. This can happen again today for those willing to take up the discipline of withdrawing into silence. Seeking silence is the beginning of spiritual maturity.

Prayerful silence can allow itself to be carried to the peak of human existence. This grace filled silence gazes on vast horizons of knowledge otherwise inaccessible to created reason. Because it cleaves to the Word of God and rests in Him, the very

---

[69] New Jerusalem Bible, (1985). Out of reverence for the Name revealed to Moses, I followed the tradition of replacing the Tetragrammaton, with "the Lord."

source of all reason, all harmony, and all mediation is opened to this kind of prayer. According to the experts of prayerful silence and this knowledge:

> The Word proceeds from Silence, and we strive to find Him in his Source. This is because the Silence here in question is not a void or a negation but, on the contrary, Being at Its fullest and most fruitful plenitude. That is why it generates; and that is why we keep silent...Books are of more value for what they do not say than for what they do. The reader is like a man gazing on a horizon. Beyond the outlines that he sees, he seeks perspectives he barely discerns, but which draw him precisely because of the mystery he senses in them. So the books one loves are those which make one think. One seeks in them that silence whence the words were born, which is those depths of soul which no language can express, for they are beyond expression. It is here we touch what is measureless, eternal and divine in us.[70]

This statement is pregnant with spiritual theology, at least in its original sense as theology flowing from a living encounter with God, and contemporary theology yearns to be filled with such mystical knowing.[71] This is why theologians should be men and women of prayer. Theology is lifeless and in fact deadly, if not infused by what is only born in attentiveness to the pregnant silence of our spiritual existence in God. Spiritual theology, in the sense that we are considering it, is interpersonal; face-to-face and heart-to-heart.

---

[70] A Carthusian, *They Speak in Silences,* Herefordshire: Gracewing: 1955, 2006, pp 5-6.
[71] This ancient notion of spiritual or mystical theology is recovered in the *Catechism of the Catholic Church* #236.

This kind of knowing is like that which lovers share. It is similar to the secret that binds true friends who have suffered together and who understand each other. Such knowing influences the whole theological conversation, changing the questions and providing ever-new levels to the answers.

St. Thomas gives us insight into this knowledge in his discussion on faith. In his explanation, to have faith means to believe in God, to believe what God says and, finally, to believe for the sake of God. This third level of faith, the level of believing for the sake of God, is directional, relational, a matter of the heart. This volitional and affective aspect to faith orients the believer to intimate friendship with God. God is not someone whom I merely believe exists or whom I merely trust is right about things. To have faith is to believe that in God is the fulfillment of all desire. The very form of faith, living faith, is charity – friendship love of God.

Faith for the sake of union with God is a response to Christ who died for our sakes. It is this dimension of faith, which is rendered in sacred silence. Silent prayer is a rendering of love in response to unsolicited, unmerited love: a love spoken in the silence of our hearts. Such great silence receives the Word with humble obedience, generously available, to whatever the Lord intends to do.

Such is the knowledge we gain by living faith in the Lord God. St. Thomas explains that this knowledge is the most certain even if it is not the clearest kind of knowing. St. John of the Cross describes it as general and obscure, but also as beautiful and as enchanting as exotic unexplored islands of some new world waiting to be discovered. English mystics call it a "cloud of unknowing." St. Gregory of Nyssa describes it as the cloud and darkness that covered Mt. Sinai at the great theophany of Moses. St. Teresa describes it as a gaze into the eyes of the One who was wounded for our sakes. For her, this knowledge is the principal cause of compunction; the water that alone quenches the gardens of our hearts. For Catherine of Siena this knowledge is gained by plunging deep into the wounds of Christ and venerating Him with kisses from his feet to his lips - the bridge from our misery to the Father's mercy. For Elisabeth of the Trinity, this knowledge is musical so that those who possess it are able to sing in their hearts the same song of praise Jesus offered to the Father on the Cross. It has the dimensions of redemptive and glorifying love.

This knowledge is a mystical aspect of theological contemplation, the most demanding and life changing of all human knowledge. All these saints are agreed that such knowledge is a sheer gift, which we can only fully receive by spending time in prayer and a life disciplined by taking our own crosses.[72] Even after 2000 years of great saints, theologians and mystics, theological contemplation remains a vast barely known frontier of human existence, for most of the inexhaustible riches of Christ are still waiting to be discovered.

Knowing God is a deeply personal encounter and makes its own demands on the way one lives life. In this loving knowledge, St. John of the Cross explains, love (not naked reasoning) leads us forward into the Divine Mystery.[73] What the intellect understands follows behind our love for the One Who discloses Himself. The loving will knows the Loving Will of God and a union of wills, each given to the other, becomes possible. This love is a friendship love: it sees the goodness and beauty of God because it has loved Him and been loved by Him first. St. Paul calls this the Wisdom of God – a gift from the Holy Spirit who searches the depths of God. (see 1 Cor.2: 6-13).

North American Pioneers for Prayer

One master of this wisdom who remains a source of renewal for the Church in North America is the Baroness, Catherine

---

[72] Ralph Martin offers a wonderful description of this kind of knowledge in his *Fulfillment of All Desire*, Steubenville: Emmaus Road (2006), 286-304.
[73] *Spiritual Canticle*,1.11, 420.

de Hueck Doherty. This political refugee from the Russian aristocracy came to Canada after World War I. Her own conversion began when the Lord saved her from starvation. With a knack for the public eye and a desire to care for the poor, she became a very popular speaker from the 1930's on. Catherine eventually started a network of ministries across America called "Friendship House."

Although these apostolates were largely successful, she realized that Americans like to be on the go all the time and we do not take enough time for silent solitude with God. She also realized that the work of evangelization and love that God was asking from her was impossible without deep prayer. Her growing hunger for contemplative silence began to change her perspective on what Americans really needed.

It was for this purpose she founded Madonna House and promoted the practice of *poustinia*.[74] She explained that *poustinia* is Russian for *deserted wilderness*. To go into *poustinia* means to allow God to allure us into a deserted place of silence and solitude for a real heart to heart encounter.

Apparently, Russians have a tradition of going into the wilderness to pray which is reminiscent of the Exodus and even the life of Christ after his Baptism. For example, the great spiritual classic, *The Way of the Pilgrim*, is based on a pilgrim who sought to live a life of prayer in the wilderness in this way. Although the rigorous asceticism described in that work might be overwhelming for most people, Catherine found a way of adapting the practice for active staff workers. She believed that this tradition would be a very important practice for overly active Americans. Most of all, she found it to be a great consolation for herself.

Deep in the Rocky Mountains lives a disciple of Catherine's who has started a retreat house called, "Our Lady of Ten-

---

[74] See her *Poustinia: Encountering God in Silence, Solitude and Prayer,* Combermere, Ontario: Madonna House (2000).

derness *Poustinia*." This *Poustinik* lived in Madonna House with the Baroness for many years and was drawn to the tradition of the *Poustinia*. Following Catherine's example, she promotes this practice and continues to welcome Christians who need a place to withdraw from the world.

Pilgrims come for a few days to a week to pray in these cozy little huts at the edge of a large forest meadow with nothing but bread, water and a Bible. At first, few of them understand what it means to be called to such a place of prayer. In a little time, however, these pilgrims discover how the silence and beauty of the holy mountain of Our Lady of Tenderness echo with the voice of God.

God created us to be in harmony with Him, with others, with nature and with ourselves. Going into silence and prayerfully entering the wilderness helps us to rediscover this harmony. But it takes time.

When in *poustinia* myself, I usually spend the first day or so of my stay drifting in and out of sleep. A little spiritually dull and insensitive to the subtle presence of God, I need a lot of rest and a little fasting before I am able to be attentive to the Lord. This is because I am over satiated with all kinds of amusements, conveniences and comforts; dissipated on all kinds of worries and anxieties; stimulated by too much news and information. Once my imagination has been deprived of the constant bombardment of artificial stimuli, and my heart has grown accustomed to waiting on the Lord, His Presence begins to disclose itself and helps me see what is essential.

Allowing the Lord to lead us into the wilderness, to those mountains where we can encounter Him, those spiritual places where silence and solitude are protected, this is vital for our life of prayer. Until we withdraw from our worldly cares, we forget how much we need the Lord. When, however, we deny ourselves and let ourselves feel a little bodily hunger, we rekindle that fundamental spiritual hunger deep within. Because it provides a place of silence and beauty, because its austerity promotes renunciation and detachment, places like the *poustinia* I visit are important for those of us who need to withdraw, feel our hunger for God, and attend to the mysterious sound of His Voice.

The Hidden Life

Historically, St. Anthony lived the final years of his life on a deserted mountain in a remote region of Egypt. It was a place that the Lord led him as an answer to his prayer for more solitude. Geographically, this mountain remains so hard to find that archeologists can only speculate as to its exact location. In fact, after his death, the body of St. Anthony was never found.

While not everyone is called to go physically into an actual desert wilderness, God has prepared a special spiritual place for us to encounter Him, a protected place where our friendship with the Lord might thrive. This spiritual place is found through the life of living faith. In this faith, a deep conversation with Jesus grows.

"Your life is hidden with Christ in God" (Col 3:3). The life of Christ is invisible to the world, an impenetrable secret to anyone whose concerns are limited to the here and now. This is in part what it means that Christ ascended into Heaven. This truth of the faith is not simply about the physical location of Christ. Heaven is much more of a state of being.

To believe that Christ ascended into heaven is to believe that He has entered into a simpler and more perfect state of being than this world can know or experience. In this earthly existence, good is subjected to futility and our ability to love one another is limited by our weakness. In Heaven, love is not obstructed by fatigue or any other limit. By entering into Heaven, Christ has raised humanity to this new state of being.

In Heaven, all the noble aspirations of human love are realized. Heaven is not something that is far from us or that we must wait to enter into only after death. It is already present by faith. Prayer accesses this new state of being, in *this* life, anticipating our life to come.

There is, however, a price: those who begin to live hidden in the mystery of faith by prayer will certainly be misunderstood by those who do not share this life. When we first begin to pray, this might be a frightening thought. Yet for those who go on the pilgrimage of prayer, they come to yearn for this secret existence, an existence that permeates the life of Christ from Bethlehem to Nazareth.

Many contemplatives of the 20th Century have come to see the hidden life of prayer as a participation in Christ's hidden life in Nazareth. Of these, Bl. Charles de Foucauld is the greatest witness by the 20th Century. A hermit evangelizing by presence in a remote mountain in the desert region of North Africa, he was recklessly shot by a frightened Islamic militant. To the world, his life looked like an utter failure: after great personal sacrifices, enduring difficult conditions for years, abandoned by everyone who promised to help, he failed to win a single convert. From his perspective, however, through faithfulness to prayer every failure became a greater participation in the hidden power of his Crucified God.

After having tried the Trappists, Charles lived as a gardener at a Poor Clare Monastery in Nazareth to learn how to enter into the hidden life of prayer. He had lived a very indulgent lifestyle until a priest talked him into going to confession. Before his confession the young military officer had questions, many of which pertained to the fervent devotion of the Muslims he had encountered during a military expedition. He wanted to be completely devoted to God like they were. Encountering the Lord by confessing his sins and doing penance, Bl. Charles discovered such devotion was possible through intimacy with, and imitation of, Christ.

The Scriptures are silent about most of the Lord's life. Jesus grew up and lived in the silent obscurity of a poor village in the rolling hills of Galilee. In Christ, God hid Himself in the anonymity of human poverty and hard work. During these mysterious years, Mary and Joseph taught Jesus to pray, to ponder within, and to attend to God.

In these hidden years, the Son of the Most High first learned to call God "Father" with His human voice and heart. The psalms became the interior language of his being while He pondered the Law and the Prophets. The disciplined life, the life of prayer, involves this same balance of obedience, simplicity of life, physical work, and study. Those who embrace this anonymity in faith discover this obscure existence to be filled with the life of God.

Bl. Charles de Foucauld understood that this experience of the ordinary things of life, an experience permeated with prayer and meditation on the words of the Holy Bible, was something the Lord had called him to in a particular way. Charles discerned that the best way to imitate this part of Christ's life was by seeking to be anonymous, to be simple, to embrace hard work, and above all, to pray without ceasing. This is how he imagined Jesus' life with Mary and Joseph.

When one lives in poverty, it is an opportunity to discover the providence of the Lord and, at the same time, an opportunity to offer up all kinds of inconveniences to God as acts of love. When some form of poverty is not a tangible inconvenience in our lives, we are robbed of such opportunities. The hidden life is something that must be chosen to act against our tendency to spiritual self-reliance or hubris. The less material comforts we choose to live with, the easier it becomes to renounce all forms of self-reliance and self-satisfaction.

By seeking the hidden life, embracing the poverty, prayer and menial labor of Jesus in Nazareth, we discover the truth about our hearts. Nazareth is an image of the human heart. Both the heart and Nazareth are places of great poverty and places where God has chosen to dwell.

In fact, our hearts are made like a void, an abyss of emptiness. This is because they have been fashioned as a dwelling place for the infinite, inexhaustible mystery of God. Christians need to order their lives so that they are not distracted from the abyss within them. Entering this abyss, suffering it, this is where we find Christ.

To enter into this mystery is to be baptized into great silence. One must make space and time for such silence. This means simplifying one's life materially and morally. Getting out of debt, cutting back on entertainment, renouncing a few creaturely comforts, these are all pathways into the hidden life if they are done for love of Jesus. Such practices lead us into a greater tenderness for those around us and they help us not be so self-preoccupied. As we do this, the Lord leads us to a hidden place, St. Anthony's inner mountain, that spiritual place where the Lord has chosen to reveal His secrets to us.

Chapter Eight

Enter the Secret Garden

Psalm 23 reveals that the life of prayer is an epic adventure that passes through tragedy to become a great romance. The Good Shepherd offers a fairytale ending in the face of the bitter vicissitudes of this life. The great wedding banquet that Christian prayer anticipates is enjoyed even now, "in the valley of death," despite the threats of one's spiritual enemies.

Christ, the Bridegroom of the soul, longs to take us into the joy of an eternal friendship where great things are accomplished for the glory of God. The garden of the Lord is a place of deepest intimacy with Him, a place where the desires of His Heart embrace the desires of our heart. Eden was such a garden. So was Gethsemane. Christ made Golgotha such a garden.

In the mystery of Christian prayer the heart is at once Golgotha and a new Eden, a place where the limits of our humanity are embraced by the limitless love of the Lord. This meeting place in prayer anticipates the New Heaven and New Earth that the Lord is fashioning, a place where every tear will be wiped dry and all the deepest aspirations of the human heart will be realized.

Some find this too fantastic to believe. It suggests that life is like a fairytale. Is it not true however that all the most joyful moments of life have the character of both anticipated but surprising ending to which even the very best fairytales merely point? And in the most intense of these moments, do they not stir our hearts a certain kind of sadness, a sorrow that knows the present joy will pass? Does not this sorrow and knowledge suggest we hope for a joy that will not pass, that deep down we hope that the fairytales are true after-all?

There is a way in which fairytales are more true to life than are the conclusions drawn from scientific study.[75] Scientific inquiry is often the effort to explain the reality of life rather than accept it. On the whole, science presumes that, when we prove a hypothesis about something, we possess its true meaning. Notwithstanding the legitimacy of this kind of knowledge, real life constantly presents solemn wonders that do not admit of explanation that can be proven. Consider, for example, those tender moments of mutual recognition provided in true friendship or the heroic sacrifices of a selfless patriot for love of country. Attempts to reduce these wonders of life to a psychological, historical or sociological explanation always fall flat. In real life, as is the case in a fairy story, one must simply accept the most beautiful parts.

Fairy stories point to the serious beauty of real life in a way that science does not. In real life and fairy stories, when rules that ought never to be broken are, it is always to the great peril of those involved. In science, on the other hand, if an event does not fit into the rule one simply develops a better rule or else ignores the anomaly. In both fairytales and real life, the broken rule must be rectified, usually by a heroic and selfless act. No body of knowledge based in the scientific method requires such sacrifice.

Here we come to one important difference between real life and fairy stories, and it is one that has nothing to do with merely historical or psychological or sociological explanations about life. In fairytales, once order is restored, the prince and the princess are married and live happily ever after. In real life, faith anticipates but does not fully realize the real happy ending because we are still in the middle of the story.

Christianity claims that, in real life, Christ has set things straight and He is coming for His Bride. Through prayer, Christians have an opportunity to share in Christ's selfless act and to

---

[75] See G.K. Chesterton's delightful work, *Orthodoxy*. J.R.R. Tolkien explores similar ideas in his work essay, *On Fairy Stories*. C.S. Lewis's experience in *Surprised by Joy* also confirms this assertion.

extend his saving power. This is what the Risen Lord invites us to in prayer. Whenever a believer chooses to do this, a deep friendship is opened up, a friendship that anticipates the happy ending the Lord is preparing at the end of time.

The unfolding of natural love is an analogy for the progress of supernatural love in us. Just as couples spend time becoming acquainted with each other before agreeing to engagement and then marriage, the Lord invites each of us to spend time with Him. The most wonderful familiarity begins to develop between the soul and God. Not only does the soul become acquainted with God and His ways, the soul becomes more and more like God the more time it spends with Him. Prayer, like the unfolding of spousal devotion, involves the progression from ardent search, to peaceful promises, to an indissoluble joy.

The joy of welcoming Christ requires that the soul pass from a kind of restlessness to a deeper peace, the peace that only knowledge of the Lord can give. This is like a betrothal, that more stable bond which friendship can enjoy only when there is deep mutual trust and a developed sense of mutual purpose. This period of betrothal, like being engaged for marriage, is itself a time of growing deeper and deeper in friendship with God.

At a certain stage, God and the soul so trust one another that they go beyond an exchange of promises to an intimate exchange of hearts. Like natural love, such an exchange is fecund. The spiritual fruit however is not limited to this life; it lasts forever.

Every real lover wants the bonds of friendship to last forever. But in this life, marriage ends with death. In other words, even the most beautiful and deepest of all human bonds – the married friendship of man and woman – falls short of the kind of relationship the Lord desires for us after natural death. Only the Lord answers the most noble and ardent of love's desires.

This present life is not big enough for the aspirations of the human heart. At the same time, there are experiences of communion in this world, so beautiful and sacred they suggest something beyond themselves. The love shared between the pilgrim Dante and his beloved Beatrice speaks to this. She rescues him from certain peril by sending him Virgil to lead him on an epic journey through hell and then she meets him in purgatory as his guide into the thresholds of heaven. Human love, though it needs to be disciplined, is ordered to higher things. Those who enter deeply into prayer believe they actually taste a love that fully anticipates that to which all other natural loves point. These mystics are convinced that the love and intimacy Christ offers in this present life is a true foretaste of that which is to come.

Just as any real friendship open to marriage is filled with beautiful adventures of the heart, mystics describe experiences of the Lord in terms of rapturous glances, tender caresses, life changing kisses, and hidden trysting places. They have this understanding because they identify themselves with the Church, the Bride of Christ. Prayer is for them a beholding of the beauty of the Beloved, heart-rending disclosures of one's deepest secrets, restless yearning in the Beloved's absence, unreserved pledges of sacrifice, and, most important of all, a kind of betrothed mutual possession which reaches for eternity. As St. John of the Cross describes it, growing in intimacy with the Lord involves being awakened by love, undertaking a great dangerous journey, being led by the Beloved to a secret place: a beautiful garden. Pursued by mortal foes who ultimately retreat before the love of the Bridegroom and his Bride, they believe the wedding feast of the Lamb is real and being unveiled to the world.

The Garden

There are many metaphors for prayer that saints and mystics have developed through the centuries, and of these, the garden is perhaps the most beautiful. Every garden has a connection with paradise: a place of order, beauty, peace and encounter with

God. Paradise is part of our primordial history. The joy, peace and simplicity that Adam and Eve enjoyed with one another and with God is the way things ought to be.

The saints have pondered the *Song of Songs*, a biblical love poem that celebrates the mystery of paradise for which every noble human love yearns. They saw this poem as a celebration not only of the love between man and woman, but in a special way, the love of God for his people, for His chosen ones. In this poem, the garden is a protected trysting place where the lovers meet one another to share their friendship.[76] When applied to the even more intimate encounter with God, many have seen the depths of the heart as a garden, a kind of paradise, a place where God and man dwell together.

When Anthony of the Desert allows God to lead him to the inner mountain, he cultivates a garden for just this purpose. The ancient eremitical ideal was that the grace of Christ restored humanity to the original friendship with God enjoyed before the Fall. Those who lived the discipline of the Christian life were walking with God in paradise once again.

The garden is also an important place of encounter for St. Augustine. In his *Confessions*, Book Eight, he discloses how the Lord rescued him from the darkness of sin and gave him the light of confidence to live the Gospel. He heard about the conversions of people less educated than he, and it stirred in him a longing and a kind of jealousy. He felt trapped. He wanted what Christianity had to offer. But could he, like they, really live it? They found the power to do so after having read a book by an Egyptian bishop, St. Athanasius about his own childhood hero.

Starting in the middle of the 4th Century, a number of Roman citizens were exposed to the writings of St. Athanasius some of which describe the life and teaching of St. Anthony. Uninspired by a culture that was becoming increasingly indulgent and turned in on itself, they were stirred by St. Anthony's freedom to

---

[76] See *Canticle of Canticles*, 4:16-5:1.

leave everything for the service of God. The secret of his freedom was a life-changing encounter with Christ. Somehow, merely by hearing about St. Anthony's experience caused them to encounter Christ as well.

What was this experience? After having lost his parents as a teenager, St. Anthony was anxious about managing the family farm and taking care of his sister. He himself had long desired to dedicate his life to prayer and the service of the Lord. Arriving at Mass just in time for the Gospel reading, he heard the story of the Rich Young Man proclaimed.

In this story, the young man wants to know how to inherit eternal life and Jesus looks on him with love and tells him to sell everything he has, to give to the poor and then to follow Him. St. Anthony discovered the Lord's look of love when he heard this passage. He sold his possessions, entrusted his sister to some elderly widows and embraced a life of prayer.

St. Augustine marveled when he learned this story and he marveled even more when he heard stories about his own contemporaries being moved by the same grace to radically follow the Lord. He was vexed. He also wanted to give up everything and radically follow the Lord. He was especially attracted to the Christian purity and the chaste lives that Christians lived. He even wanted to embrace total continence, especially because he saw this as a way of entering more deeply into intellectual fellowship with others. He yearned for the joy of living together in common in a way of life that would promote intellectual contemplation.

The problem was sex. By this time in his life, he had been living with a woman for years and even had a son outside of wedlock. The thought of life without regular sexual intimacy unsettled him. He was afraid that if he chose to follow the Lord, he would not be able to handle it. Could he really live without the joys of sexual pleasure? On the other hand, he could no longer stand the thought of continuing to live as he had. He knew he

141

needed something more. Finally, he understood that only the Lord could provide such a grace, and the only way to get it was to humble himself and ask.

He ran to a garden to be alone, and begged the Lord in tears. There is a reason why Saint Augustine tells his readers about this detail. Gardens are special places of encounters with the Lord – not only the Garden of Eden but also the Garden in front of the empty tomb where Mary Magdalene met the Lord. In his garden, he would learn a great secret that would free him, allow him to live with himself (*habitare secum*), and allow him to embrace conversion of life (*conversatio morum*). In the intimacy of a garden, he pours his heart out to the Lord begging for the grace to make a new beginning, and he hears a voice commanding him to read the Bible. When he obeyed the voice, he felt as though the Lord spoke to him directly through the words of the Bible in the same way St. Anthony did. Only the words he read were from Romans 13:15: "Make no provision for the flesh."

Like St. Anthony, the effect of this encounter with Jesus through a Biblical passage was immediate. St. Augustine says that the light of God's confidence flooded his soul. The darkness and the doubt were no more. He clung to the Word of the Lord Whom the words of Sacred Scripture had revealed.

The Heart as a Garden

Teresa of Avila describes beginning to pray in terms of cultivating a garden. The garden she has in mind is the most intimate of all settings: the heart. After her own conversion, she read Augustine's *Confessions* and his experience helped her understand her own. She also realized that in order to realize the deepest desires of her heart, she had to rely on the Lord alone. The only way to do this was by intimacy with Christ in prayer. He alone has the power to overcome those things that hold us back.[77]

---

[77] See *Book of her Life*, Chapter 7.

Teresa taught we must do everything we can so that He can make our hearts beautiful.[78] The heart is meant to be a beautiful place of encounter with the Lord. This makes sense. In the depths of our hearts, Christ is the soil from which all life springs, and at the same time He is the water of everlasting life. His deepest desire is that our hearts would burst forth with life and beauty and fruitfulness. When we work with Him to help Him realize his desire, it gives Him even greater joy.

How do we help Christ make the garden of our heart beautiful? We have already discussed the virtues of humility and courage when we first considered the conversion of Teresa of Avila. She describes inner strength and readiness to accept the truth as beautiful and fragrant flowers especially enjoyed by Christ as He comes into our hearts. In this discussion, we want to focus on that which causes such beauty to grow in the heart.

The answer she proposes concerns the effort to stir feelings of devotion for Christ. She is convinced the shedding of tears whether physically or spiritually disposes the heart to mental prayer or contemplation. Tears of compunction are like water for the garden of our heart. Compunction in fact means to be pierced to the heart. In order to pray, we need to do whatever we can to make ourselves vulnerable to the love of Jesus. Only when we open wide the doors of our hearts to Him does He have the freedom to act in our lives.

She recommends two principle activities for disposing ourselves to feelings of devotion. We can think about Jesus and various scenes of His life or we can carefully examine our lives and search for His presence in our memories. They are both forms of meditation open to moments of deep intimacy with Jesus that center our powers of imagination, understanding and affectivity on the Lord and help us become mindful of Him.

In very gentle and profound ways, sometimes noticed and sometimes not, He touches us when we try to exercise sincere and

---

[78] See *Book of her Life*, Chapter 11.

mindful devotion. As we call to mind the Passion of the Christ, the thought of Him who was pierced for our offenses also pierces us. As we call to mind His mercy in our lives, we find countless instances of His kindness for which the only proper response is sober gratitude and adoration.

Beginning to pray for Teresa of Avila involves attentiveness to the presence of God. In her own efforts to be attentive to Him, she meditated on Christ within her or read a spiritual book to place herself in the presence of God. While doing this, she would oftentimes experience the Lord suddenly making Himself felt in such a way that she could no longer doubt that He was in her or that she was totally immersed in Him. She sometimes even felt suspended outside herself in love unable to remember or think about anything but Him. She explained that the only understanding of this she enjoyed was that she knew she understood nothing about it. His presence was too immense, too beautiful, and too intimate to understand. She identifies this experience as "mystical theology."[79]

In this knowledge, the heart piercing presence of the Lord often caused her to cry. This spiritual water helped her pray and helped her grow in virtue. She learned that, although in the beginning drawing up this spiritual water took a lot of effort and determination, at a certain stage it became easier and easier for her to rest in the loving awareness of God's presence. She called this ability to rest in God's presence, the Prayer of Quiet. Such prayer is the holy recollection of the powers of our soul in Christ, a silent stillness before the mystery of His presence, and an adoring openness to His generous love. It is like standing at the threshold of heaven. In her reflection on the Lord's Prayer, St. Teresa turns our attention to the immanent presence of our heavenly Father:

---

[79] *Book of her Life*, chapter 10.1, in *Collected Works*, vol. 1, translators Kieran Kavanaugh O.C.D., and Otilio Rodriguez O.C.D., Washington D.C.: ICS (1976, second edition rev. 1987) 105.

You already know that God is everywhere. It's obvious, then, that where the king is there is his court; in sum, wherever God is, there is heaven. Without a doubt you can believe that where His Majesty is present, all glory is present... All one need do is go into solitude and look at Him within oneself, and not turn away from so good a Guest but with great humility speak to Him as to a father. Beseech Him as you would a father; tell Him about your trials; ask Him for a remedy against them, realizing that you are not worthy.[80]

Along the same line St. John of the Cross encourages:

What more do you want, O soul! And what else do you search for outside, when within yourself you possess your riches, delights, satisfaction, fullness and kingdom – your Beloved whom you desire and seek? Be joyful and gladdened in your interior recollection with Him, for you have Him so close to you. Desire Him there, adore Him there.[81]

The Practice of Mental Prayer

The key for beginning to pray, as Teresa of Avila understands it, is to learn to attend to the Lord, to focus the heart on the things of God. A holy picture or the Bible or a good book on prayer can free us from distractions as we turn our hearts to the Lord. Then, closing our eyes, we can think about holy things again, and these thoughts are already the beginning of prayer, mental prayer. In all likelihood, anyone reading this book has en-

---

[80] *Way of Perfection*, 28.1 in *Collected Works*, vol. 2, 140-141.
[81] *Spiritual Canticle*, 1.8 in *Collected Works of John of the Cross*, trans Otilio Rodriguez O.C.D. and Kieran Kavanaugh O.C.D., Washington, D.C.: ICS (1991) 480.

tered into the experience of such prayer even without being fully aware that such thoughts are in fact the beginning of prayer.

This was the case of St. Thérèse of Lisieux who was told that she should not practice mental prayer because she was so young. However, she loved to think about heaven and would try to find quiet places where she could do this and not be disturbed. In boarding school, one of the Sisters found her deep in such thought. She asked little Thérèse what she was doing. Therese explained that she was not praying but merely thinking about heaven. The wise old religious told the Little Flower to keep up those thoughts.

Mental prayer is almost always possible when we are honest with ourselves. This is true even when our hearts do not seem to feel what they should when we think about holy things. Consider the Christ dying for us on the Cross. Some who think of this are immediately moved with tears and gratitude, as was Teresa of Avila eventually. Often, however, where there should be profound gratitude, we feel repulsion. This repulsion is a profound poverty. We know what we should feel, but we do not feel it. If you feel this, do not be discouraged. Lift up your heart. It is precisely in this poverty that we should begin to seek Christ's love.

Entering the Double Abyss

Blessed Elisabeth of the Trinity, born Elisabeth Catez, loved spending hours searching for the Lord in her heart. She rarely writes about feeling this Presence or even imagining it. This is because she found the presence on a deeper level than the imagination or the emotions can perceive.

In faith, she begs Christ to fascinate her, to fixate her, to envelop her, and to establish her in peace. The Presence of the Lord she enjoyed the most was His Presence in faith. It was this kind of presence of Christ that she found to be life changing. Blessed Elisabeth traveled the pathway to this garden of faith through descent into what she called the double abyss: the abyss of our misery and the abyss of God's mercy.[82]

Elisabeth had to deal with a fiery temper. Although she was very loving and very devoted to prayer from an early age, gentleness did not come easy for her. She felt movements of anger that sometimes threatened her most important relationships with family and friends. She was experiencing the misery of our humanity, the absence of an original love we were meant to know, one we ought to have had, but are no longer able to enjoy.

This misery, this absence, gave birth to our primordial lack of interior harmony. This we experience in very personal and difficult ways. For Blessed Elisabeth, as for many who want to serve the Lord, this misery expressed itself in an explosive lack of gentleness.

Many people get to a place in their spiritual life where they get frustrated because of a shortcoming in their character that is difficult to change. They see their weaknesses, but unfortunately, they do not always see God's love. It is God's love, however, and not our failure, that most characterizes our existence. The secret of doing something beautiful for God is to believe in God's love more than one's own weakness.

Blessed Elisabeth, rather than run away from her weakness, came to see her struggles as opportunities to rely on God in a deeper way. Her moments of struggle put her in touch with the misery she suffered deep in her heart because she learned to use them to turn to the Lord in prayer. Blessed Elisabeth's writings are filled with a beautiful wisdom one only learns by suffering the truth about how God works. Conversion to Christ does not make our misery magically go away. In her writings, one's misery is the pathway to Christ.

One descends this pathway by holy recollection, silent attentiveness to the Lord. In this prayer, one is wholly vigilant for

---

[82] See her retreat written for her sister, a married lay woman, *Heaven in Faith*, #4.

Christ as one descends into the absence of love in the human heart. One encounters in this descent all kinds of darkness, sorrow and pain; all of which threaten and weigh down the spirit.

The slope of holy recollection slides into this abyss of misery. The reason for this journey, however, is not to wallow in self-pity; rather, it is a search for Christ. If we persevere in this search, we discover the abyss of His mercy. He suffers what we lack in our hearts with us so that we might turn to Him and rely on His power in our weakness.

As Elisabeth turned to prayer, she was overwhelmed by the Lord's presence in her own misery: bearing her up, suffering her lack of love with her, and restoring her dignity. Borrowing language from other mystics, she called this encounter with God's mercy in her misery the divine impact.[83] Her misery was limited by God's mercy just as a weaker force is contained by a more powerful impulse.

In prayer, she discovered the surging sea of divine love crashing in on her emptiness. In the face of the immensity of God's overwhelming love, she was able to let go of her old way of life, including her fiery temper. Her lack of gentleness suffered a mystical death that God's gentleness might begin to reign. In prayer she discovered a mortification of her irrational inner impulses by which the she might live by love.

After she became a Carmelite nun, she was convinced that this encounter of the Lord in the heart was essential not only for priests and religious but also the lay faithful. She wrote a retreat in which she counsels her married sister, a mother of young children; "The divine impact occurs in the deepest depths, where the abyss of our nothingness touches the Abyss of mercy, the whole totality of God's immensity. There we will find strength to die to ourselves and, losing all vestige of self, we will be changed into love."[84]

---

[83] See for example her *Letter 335* to Sr. Marie-Odile.

[84] *Heaven in Faith*, #5, my own paraphrase for emphasis.

Seeking God in nothingness as Elisabeth describes rings with primordial overtones of creation. Prayer takes on the proportions of a new creation, where the chaotic vestiges of an ego alienated from God are lost and a new identity rooted in the very reality of God is established. The all of God, the totality of His immensity, is known in the human heart through encountering divine mercy. The search for the Lord within is the effort to find those places in the substance of the soul where God's mercy and human misery touch each other, where one has bearing on the other.

The Experience of a Young Priest

A young priest from Houston shared a beautiful story that illustrates this transforming dimension of prayer. In a homily to a group of distinguished scholars gathered at the local seminary, he told about his escape from Vietnam as a young boy on a small crowded boat, which lacked sufficient food and water. On the boat, there was a small child and his mother, a pregnant woman separated from her husband. They faced near starvation and severe dehydration until their boat landed on shore. As soon as they arrived, the poor woman died, and a makeshift funeral was held for her. He remembered the little boy crawling onto his mother and repeating over and over again, "Mommy wake up."

This memory was filled with righteous indignation towards God. How could God allow something like this to happen to an innocent little child? Could not God have done something?

Years later this young man was in formation for the priesthood. He went on a long retreat at the Institute of Priestly Formation in Creighton, Nebraska. It was warm and he was taking a swim. Something about the water reminded him of his experience those many years before and he felt that anger towards the Lord return. It was just at this moment that he was drawn into deep prayer, and he had to stop swimming and stand still in the water.

When the Lord speaks His Word in the heart, His Word surpasses our language, so that whatever words we use to express what we believe is said to us are primarily descriptive of what was communicated. Teresa of Avila describes this phenomenon throughout her own writings on prayer and provides the impression that this sort of communication is not uncommon among those who have begun to pray. The experience is often associated with mystical contemplative prayer. In fact, the *Catechism of the Catholic Church* calls contemplation a kind of listening to the silence of God.[85]

The young priest went on to explain what the Lord spoke in his heart. He saw the dead mother again and the little child begging her to wake up. Only this time, he saw something else which pierced him to the heart and put his righteous indignation towards God to rest. The woman and her child were being held in the lap of Jesus. He described how the Lord looked at him with a humble rebuke in his eyes. The painful memory was not taken away. Instead, it was transformed from an occasion of bitterness towards God into a fountain of hope – because in prayer, the young priest had discovered the merciful presence of the Lord in his misery.

Habitare secum – living with oneself and interior deliberation[86]

Is it really important to consider our nothingness when we look for the Lord's merciful presence in our lives? Those who seek the Presence of the Lord in the dark places of their hearts

---

[85] See ##2716-2717.

[86] Like other ideas in the Rule of St. Benedict, *habitare secum* is not easily translated. The concept is closely tied with the pledge of *conversatio morum* which comes up in the same paragraph. Before one joins the community by pledging obedience, stability, and ongoing conversion (*conversatio morum*), a candidate is to spend some time being tested, learning the *Rule* and living with himself (*habitare secum*). See *Rule of St. Benedict*, #58.

learn the secret of *habitare secum,* the secret of living with oneself. There are such dark places in our lives; only with the mercy of the Lord can we face ourselves and deal with the reality of who we really are.

This ideal began to be articulated around the time of St. Benedict, although it was a lived part of Christian spirituality from the very beginning. It means not only confessing sin and doing penance for the evil that one has done, but also accepting one's weaknesses and learning to offer one's limitations to God. Most especially *habitare secum* means being able to enter into the depths of one's own heart to humbly listen to the Lord who waits for us there.

Christian prayer deals with the reality of the human heart. The heart is the spring from which flows good and evil. It is broken and wounded, laden with many sorrows, and yet still capable of finding joy in what is good. It is an inner sanctuary where God speaks to us. People who do not want to deal with themselves or deal with God do not like to go there. They remain unfamiliar to themselves and unaware of what is driving them in life. Yet, when God calls us to Himself and we begin to yearn to be with Him, entering into our hearts, accepting what is there and offering it to the Lord are the best ways to find Him.

The reason why has to do with the theme of mercy Pope Benedict singled out in his homily at the beatification of John Paul II: mercy is the limit of evil. John Paul II loved the theme of Divine Mercy. It was the mercy of God that helped him deal with the cruel brutality of World War II which was followed by decades of Soviet oppression.

Blessed John Paul was convinced that Divine Mercy is the limit of evil because the more he trusted in Jesus, the more he saw the triumph of mercy. Contemplating the face of Christ and clinging to the mercy of God was the secret not only of dealing with himself but also of being merciful to others, even those who tried to kill him. His confidence in Divine Mercy made John Paul II a compelling advocate for the dignity of the human person which is why people were drawn to him all over the world.

Evil, the mystery of sin, dehumanizes, but Divine Mercy raises on high! Mercy is love that suffers the misery of another, the evil that afflicts someone's heart, so that the dignity of that person might be restored. On the Cross, Christ embraced our misery so that we might know God's mercy.

The good and evil we find in the heart are *not* co-equal principles: good has definitively triumphed over evil in the death and resurrection of Jesus Christ. When we turn to Him in faith, He gives us the power of His mercy and teaches us to realize the victory of good over evil in our lives. He has already suffered our misery with us and is ever ready to meet us there; so that in Him all that is good, noble and true about us is rescued from the mystery of sin and raised up to new life.

To learn to live with ourselves - this is to look at those places in our lives where evil has a foothold, and offering them to God so that we can realize in ourselves how Divine Mercy is the limit of evil. If the abyss of our misery is deep, the abyss of mercy is inexhaustibly deeper. The One crucified by love bears with us the absence of love, the misery, with which we are afflicted so that, by our union in his suffering, we are constantly more deeply established is His love—a love which surpasses every sin, limitation, privation, failure, and weakness.

The more we discover this limit to the evil in our own hearts, the more we can rejoice in the remarkable and astonishing presence of the Lord in our lives. Rather than being driven by all kinds of brokenness we do not understand, we find ourselves able to live like St. Benedict, Bl. John Paul II and the other great saints, who through such interior deliberation discovered the secret of living with themselves before the face of God. *Habitare secum* is an interior search for the Mercy of the Lord.

Dryness in Prayer

Saint Teresa explains that we should expect aridity, dislike, and distaste for prayer in the beginning. Sometimes, even the very advanced go through these experiences. This is like lowering the bucket into the well and appearing to pull it up empty. When hard work seems to bear no fruit, she advises us that our efforts are not in vain. She admonishes us to keep our eyes focused confidently on Him, the Lord of the Garden, even when we are utterly exhausted in prayer. Our tears are not as pleasing to the Lord as is our effort and humility.

After describing beginning to pray as drawing up water from a well, Saint Teresa goes on to explain the prayer of quiet and other kinds of contemplation. A few comments on the prayer of quiet will help us understand what God is doing when we begin to take up mental prayer. The Prayer of Quiet helps us put into context the difficult struggles and frustrations that afflict us when we first get started. By understanding this stage of prayer, we will be able to begin with more patience and hope.

Teresa explains that prayer becomes easier as we acquire the habit of recollection. Indeed, we become more comfortable not only with God but also with ourselves. The ancient practice of *habitare secum* informs our existence. Being at peace with ourselves to a minimal degree, we begin to experience better self-control and awareness of the sweetness of God.

To describe how this kind of prayer is different from the simple efforts we make to meditate on Christ or our efforts to search for Christ hidden in the difficult parts of our lives, she uses the image of a windlass pumping water. When we first begin to pray, we water our garden drawing water with a bucket. That is, we work hard to think about the Lord and what He has done for us.

This effort can be exhausting and tedious at first. The problem is that we are not sure what we want. The Lord attracts

153

us but our heart is still divided. But after a time of drawing the refreshing water of Christ, we become more and more confident about what we really want. The powers of our soul begin to coalesce around Him.

Rather than pulling water out of a well with a bucket, once the habit of prayerfulness is formed in us, it is as if we have a spiritual hand-pump drawing devotion from our hearts. Some mistake this recollection for a detached self-satisfied mental state which escapes into a disingenuous piety and sits in judgment over everyone else. Real recollection does not admit of such aggression. On the contrary, the heart habitually recollected in quiet prayerfulness and submitting itself to the voice of Christ is sober, humble and deeply compassionate.

Those who have learned to recollect their powers in the Lord suffer from hunger and thirst for spiritual things, and long for the peace only the Lord can give. They do not feel worthy of the Lord's love and yet their thoughts are always turned towards Him. Compassionate towards the suffering and weaknesses of others, their ardent desire for the Lord does not allow them to be as judgmental as they once were. Less divided in their desires and more focused on Jesus, the prayerfully recollected constantly seek more silence in their lives and ache for Him all the time.

The Beginning of Mystical Prayer

As our garden begins to grow, St. Teresa speaks of an even more refreshing kind of prayer. This kind of prayer does not involve our labor. In this prayer, the Lord captures our hearts with love. At first, it is just a little spark, but a spark which can ignite a raging fire. She says the Lord captures our will. Deep inside, there is a yearning for the Lord that begins to form our life. With this spark of prayer, the garden of our heart is watered more quickly and effectively.

We experience a cry of the heart that does not come from ourselves. It is the Holy Spirit praying in us Himself in a way of which we are barely aware. Movements of gratitude and contrition ring in our depths like a heartbeat. This is because the Lord is present to us in a new way and his love continues to capture our hearts. We feel joyfully grateful, and, at the same time, we realize how cold we have been to Him. This realization pierces us with a holy sorrow. Contrition and gratitude are great gifts God yearns to pour out in our hearts.

Higher levels of prayer in St. Teresa's writings include the image of canals and finally rain that comes from God. As the feelings of devotion flow in deeper and more intense ways, the spark of mystical prayer grows into a flame, and this flame, if safeguarded by a disciplined life, roars into a blazing fire. The point is that beginning to pray, if we are faithful, disposes us to these other kinds of prayer in which God is active. Our perseverance and determination create an environment in our hearts where He is free to work. Our openness to this work allows Him to transform our inner depths, to stir us with love.

There is one important observation to make about the garden of the heart and these experiences of prayer described by Teresa of Avila. She notes from her own experience that it is quite possible for someone to have very advanced experiences in prayer but still be very spiritually immature. No matter how advanced someone's life of prayer, it is utterly meaningless if it is not joined with a growth in virtue. The whole reason for all the beautiful experiences Christ gives is that our souls should become beautiful with the works of His love – those spiritual dispositions that are always ready to reveal His glory.

In our consumerist society, there are many who approach prayer with a spiritual insobriety and gluttony. In their anxiety to achieve psychic states or experience extraordinary mystical phenomena, they miss the whole point of prayer, which is union with

God—not the acquisition and consumption of spiritual experiences. They have come to a banquet but ignored the Host.

Though they are behaving like swine, the Lord loves them and allows them to suffer difficult spiritual afflictions so that in their dryness they might discover room in their hearts for a deeper love. The Host deprives them only so that they might turn their eyes to Him once again and discover the true reason for the wedding feast to which they have been called.

There is one final observation for a correct understanding of St. Teresa's Degrees of Prayer. Even though there is a certain progress from one kind of prayer to another, it should not be assumed that mystical contemplation is only given to those in acquired recollection or the Prayer of Quiet. St. Teresa was surprised and even concerned that she sometimes was taken deep into mystical prayer even while she was assailed by all kinds of distracting thoughts and fantasies.

Meditation and recollected silence can dispose to mystical contemplation, but they are not required for it. Not even feelings of devotion or tears of compunction are required. This is because in this higher form of prayer the Holy Spirit is praying in us. Sometimes He also moves our intellect, imagination and emotions. He is, however, sovereign to move how and where He wills. All the Lord needs is our ardent effort to be faithful, to cleave to Him by living faith. He is ever ready to do His part when we make the least bit of effort to do ours.

Chapter Nine

Theological Contemplation

Although today theological study is often reduced to a highly technical communication of vast amounts of information, in the broader history of the Church, the study of God and all things in relation to Him has been associated with prayer. *The Nine Ways of Prayer* of St. Dominic suggests edifying connections between prayer and study, contemplation and preaching. Both prayer and study seek, after all, a Living God who is never static or passive but eternally active and dynamic.

Prayer is theological and prayerful study of the Word made flesh is essentially Christian. The study of sacred doctrine can include moments in which wings of love bear us to the heights of mystical prayer while, even in the same moment, we are gripped with silent wonder in kneeling adoration over the astonishing ways the Lord manifests Himself. Here, prayerful reflection laden with compunction can surge like a wave onto whole new shores of intellectual insight gained by disciplined study. These movements of heart and mind so permeate each other in the Dominican tradition that St. Thomas Aquinas distinguishes but does not separate the wisdoms gained in prayerful study.

Contemplation has a wide range of meanings for St. Thomas.[87] It can be the simple act of reasoning from one point to

---

[87] To study, to know, to behold, to see – these activities are all related to contemplation. The Angelic Doctor begins to unfold these meanings in the beginning of the *Summa Theologica* when he asks whether Sacred Doctrine is a science (I q.1, a.2). He understands the Dominican vocation as taking up into a single way of life both contemplation and preaching (see II-II, q188, aa.5-6). Theology or Sacred Doctrine and Natural Theology or what we now call Philosophy of God are complementary, the former dealing with revealed Truth and the

the next.[88] It can be an angelic vision of reality spiraling around itself.[89] Contemplation can also be a simple gaze, which sees and appreciates the whole.[90] This activity can be simply natural or else produced under the impetus of the Holy Spirit who provides supernatural knowledge, understanding and wisdom.[91]

Such mystical contemplation produces great joy and is always given for some important purpose.[92] For the Angelic Doctor, such experiences can be occasioned by the study of sacred doctrine.[93] In fact, the word *contemplatio* in Latin can simply mean "to study" but also carries connotations of, and even presumes, even deeper intellectual acts produced by God.

A Humanizing Influence on Society

Does contemplation thwart social progress? As personal a pursuit as theological contemplation might seem, it is a driving force for human history. The Medieval University emerged from this kind of pursuit of the truth and with it the advancement of Western Civilization as a whole. Not only were some the greatest artistic achievements known to man produced in the prayer-

---

later dealing with what can be known by nature. In formal study, we distinguish these efforts as does St. Thomas. He comes back to this idea again when he asks how God is known by us (I, q.12, a.5-13). In the life of prayer, it is possible that one's natural contemplation of God as manifest in what He has made dances with a consideration of what He has revealed in a manner which disposes one to the operation of the gifts of knowledge, understanding and wisdom all at once. For more on the gifts particularly related to contemplation see II-II, qq.8, 9, and 45.

[88] See his treatment of reasoning and understanding (ways we "behold" reality) as one power of the soul, *Summa Theologica* I, q.79, a.8.

[89] *Summa Theologica* II-II, q180, a. 6.

[90] Same as above.

[91] *Summa Theologica*, II-II, qq.8, 9, and 45

[92] *Summa Theologica*, I q.43, aa.5and6.

[93] Compare *Summa Theologica*, I q.1, a.6, reply 3, II-II, q.43 and II-II, q. 188, a. 5.

imbued culture of Christendom, but also many of the greatest scientists, statesmen and saints.

Has the contemporary abandonment of contemplative wisdom improved society? Dare we question the thesis that theology imbued with mystical wisdom hinders the human development of society? What is technical advancement if we have lost our humanity in the process?

A culture of life and civilization of love grow when the soil of humanity is exposed to the radiance of God. It is to this radiance that contemplative prayer rooted in sacred doctrine exposes humanity so that we might work for a better humanism than is currently guiding the public square. Society needs the development of a truly Christian humanism—an understanding of humanity in the light of the Gospel of Christ.

Towards a Theology Knelt in Adoration[94]

In order to be a compelling force in social renewal, theological wisdom needs the animating power of mystical wisdom and study of theology needs to be imbued with a deeper contemplation of the Word made flesh. Some presume that recourse to prayer in the context of theological study is anti-intellectual, a flight into fantasy or even an escape into the merely affective. Such prejudice indicates a disconcerting shift in the nature of theological study.

Theologians of every age have striven to bring theological questions to light in a scientific and disciplined way. A scientific inquiry brings one's personal awareness of sacred doctrine into the highest level of rational consciousness, a level at which mutual understanding can be arrived at. Yet, for the most part, only in

---

[94] Hans Urs von Balthasar underscored the importance of a kneeling theology, a theology in which one's personal sanctity and scholarship are submitted to the sanctifying Word of God. See, for example, "Theology and Sanctity," in *Word and Redemption. Essays in Theology* 2 (English trans., New York: 1965) 49-86.

the modern and post-modern eras has such theological wisdom been pursued without regard for mystical wisdom.

It is time to return to a theology studied on one's knees. Our greater awareness of method and recourse to technology in theology today seems to be at the expense of prayer. Very few scholars teach or write as if they believe that contemplation is of any objective value to the theological enterprise or that mystical wisdom has any real importance for the life of the Church. At least this is the impression one gets from what is published in many academic periodicals. Can theology without prayer build up the holiness of the Church?

St. John of the Cross's Theological Vision

This problem began to raise its head in 16th Century Spain. Members of the Inquisition and some bishops had come to the opinion that mental prayer was dangerous. This meant that for many people throughout Spanish society, the spiritual life was limited to basic catechesis, external liturgical practice, recitation of vocal prayers and the practice of moral virtue. In the meantime, many were deprived of the deeper devotion to Christ which contemplative prayer makes possible. The Carmelite Reform would be the main cultural force renewing both the Church and the broader society.

St. John of the Cross lost his father at an early age and grew up in poverty. Yet, despite these difficult conditions, his family was filled with love. He loved to sing, go on hikes, camp in the wilderness, minister to the sick and spend time in prayerful solitude. By Divine Providence, he was provided good schooling under the early Jesuits where he cultivated aptitudes in the liberal and fine arts, especially poetry and theology.

His education grounded him in a sound humanism and understanding of the Sacred Scriptures. Although prayer and theology were separated in the academy, he was convinced that sacred doctrine and contemplation belonged together. St. Teresa of Avila convinced him to bring these convictions to bear on the Carmelite reform she had begun.

He became a priest of considerable administrative ability and a spiritual director of extraordinary gifts. He not only helped lead the Carmelite reform during a dangerous period, even enduring imprisonment, but he also established houses of formation and all kinds of ministries. No stranger to politics, his insistence on fairness and kindness caused him to be misunderstood, rejected and persecuted. Even so, this did not discourage the rigorous schedule of spiritual direction that he maintained for priests, nuns and the lay faithful. Promoting contemplative prayer was his primary mission.

To help those entrusted to his spiritual guidance, he composed beautiful poetry by which he would teach important doctrines for the life of prayer. In his writings there are references and explanations of what we deem to be theological contemplation, a kind of prayer that takes place deep in the heart. One of his most thought provoking descriptions of this kind of prayer is linked to the beginning of mystical contemplation:

> O Spring like crystal!
> If only, on your silvered-over faces,
> You would suddenly form
> the eyes I have desired,
> which I bear sketched deep within my heart.[95]

This ardent prayer, this deep desire emerges in the midst of theological refection. It represents for St. John of the Cross a milestone in the ascent of the hidden mountain and entrance into the secret garden of contemplation. We have already seen how he begins the Spiritual Canticle by describing a spiritual awakening in terms of an ardent lover pleading with her beloved to show

---

[95] St. John of the Cross, *Spiritual Canticle*, stanza 12, *Complete Works*, 515.

himself. From this John of the Cross goes on to describe the journey of a soul searching for Christ in terms of the messengers He sends and the enemies which must be faced. Here, he takes us to the threshold of a deeper encounter, a tender face to face, a reflection on sacred doctrine that leads to a more mature union with God.

Sacred Doctrine as a Living Fount for Prayer

The soul who withdraws to seek God dwelling in its depths contains a fountain of living water according to St. John of the Cross. This image speaks to the beauty of the truths of the faith received into the heart. They have the quality of water which in stillness becomes smooth. The more fully sacred doctrine is received into one's life, the more peaceful or smoother theology becomes to reflect on.

Beyond a simple mental assent to theological facts, receiving these teachings means to allow them to pierce through our dull indifference and so that we might treasure them as a gift from a friend. How we treat the gift reveals our attitude toward the giver. Applying oneself to the study of sacred doctrine with grateful devotion purifies and strengthens our faith. St. John of the Cross is describing this inner purity when he speaks about the surface of these waters being smooth like crystal and as reflective as silver. [96]

What is sought in this reflection and how it is sought constitutes the essential character of theological contemplation. One who is deeply in love thinks about her beloved all the time and, when he cannot be found, yearns to glimpse his eyes in every re-

---

[96] St. Thomas Aquinas explains this purifying effect of contemplation in terms of the operation of the infused gifts of knowledge, understanding and wisdom. See *Summa Theologica*, II-II, qq. 8, 9, and 45.

flection. Those who ponder the truths of our faith filled with longing for Christ yearn for them to yield a sign of His presence.[97]

The Reflective Quality of Sacred Doctrine

The reflective quality of the water describes an essential characteristic of the sacred doctrine that waters the heart. St. Thomas Aquinas says that the articles of faith are truth-bearing: they bear relation to the First Truth who is God.[98] St. John of the Cross brings this insight to bear on St. Paul's description that we "see" by faith "dimly" as in "a mirror." [99] In the Carmelite's description of the role of Sacred Doctrine in prayer, faith finds the revelation of the Truth Himself reflected in the articles of the faith as in a mirror.

St. John of the Cross's teaching helps explain Anthony Bloom's remarkable encounter with the Lord while he read the Gospel of Mark. It also helps to account for the enthusiasm we witnessed in Denver during the liturgies of World Youth Day, '93. Both of these cases suggest the relation that the sacred doctrine of our faith bears to the presence of the Lord. The Lord's presence is accessible to us in propositions of our faith, not with the clarity provided by our natural power of understanding, but obscurely, dimly as if in a reflection.

Sacred doctrine is essential for the spiritual life because it makes it possible to gaze on Christ Himself. The more we study

---

[97] See *Spiritual Canticle*, 12.5 and 13.2, *Complete Works*, 517-520. Bl. John Paul II, in his doctoral dissertation at the Angelicum, explains that the description of the Lord's presence in doctrine is noteworthy because "it stimulates a vehement desire to see..." *Faith according to Saint John of the Cross*, trans. Jordan Aumann, San Francisco: Ignatius Press (1981, reprinted 1985, 1986) 210. Theological contemplation is nothing other than a gaze into doctrine motivated by this desire.

[98] See *Summa theologica* II-II, 1.1. Probably the most compelling explanation of this is that provided by Romanus Cessario, *The Virtue of Faith and the Theologal Life*, Washington, D.C.:CUA (1996), 63-76.

[99] See 2 Corinthians 3:18.

the faith with devotion of heart, the more we expose ourselves to wonder and awe before the Lord. Over and above what we understand theologically, prayerful reflection on what we believe gives a loving general knowledge of Him in a personal and intimate manner.

The "eyes" of the Lord formed in this reflection stir intense desires in the heart according to the Carmelite Master. In other words, it is possible to be deeply moved, profoundly shaken when in our efforts to ponder our faith we catch the Lord's piercing love reflected in them. St. John describes this presence of Christ as no less than "remarkable." [100] Sacred doctrine, far from remaining on the level of abstract speculation, reflects the gaze of *Someone* who looks on us with love. When "sketched deep within" the heart, this kind of knowledge occasions spiritual maturity.[101]

The Anagogical Act –
Mysteriously drawn by the Lord's ineffable beauty

This knowledge described as sketched deep within the heart is not immediately accessible by means of conscious rational reflection. If death is deeper than our conscious awareness, this loving knowledge penetrates even deeper into the substance of the soul. This knowledge, a tender mutual recognition of love, makes us vulnerable to our own mystery, the question our own existence poses to us.

---

[100] *Spiritual Canticle*, 12.5, *Complete Works*, 517.

[101] *Spiritual Canticle*, 12.6, *Complete Works*, 517. "Sketched" is contrasted with a completed painting in this passage, as a way of describing how this kind of knowledge is not yet beatific vision, but an anticipation of it, something that will come to completion when we pass out of the light of faith given in this life into the light of glory offered in the next. This experience, this knowledge, in the context of the poem, causes a soul to move from the yearning but unsettled desires with which one begins the spiritual life into a more peaceful and confident friendship love – qualities that indicate proficiency in following the Lord.

What is it that God recognizes in us when we discover his loving gaze? To be made in the image of God is to be a creature of mysterious proportions. We have been fashioned with spiritual centers so vast and deep that they exceed the capacity of our own natural powers to ever exhaust.

If we cannot consciously know them, how do we know these unfathomable depths really exist at all? In the end, it is a matter of faith. Faith is the evidence of things not seen.[102] God alone knows and loves the deepest truth of our existence with a love stronger than death. It is to these mysterious depths that knowledge of the love of God is meant to take us:

> Passing beyond all that is naturally and spiritually intelligible or comprehensible, souls ought to desire with all their might to attain what in this life could never be known or enter the human heart... In this way, in obscurity, souls approach union swiftly by means of faith, which is also dark. And in this way gives them wondrous light.[103]

By faith we seek and find what we cannot see by reason alone: the mysterious knowledge of the glory of God in the face of Christ.[104] This is mystical knowledge. The soul that possesses this finds less satisfaction in what it understands this is about the faith than in what it does not understand: the ineffable incomprehensibility of Divine Love:

> Look at the infinite knowledge and that hidden secret. What peace, what love, what silence is in that divine bosom! How lofty the science God teaches there, which is

---

[102] *Hebrews* 11:1. See also St. Thomas Aquinas, *Summa Theologica*, II-II, 4.1.

[103] St. John of the Cross, *Ascent of Mount Carmel*, book 2, 4, 6; *Complete Works*, 161.

[104] See 2 *Corinthians* 4:6 and 18.

what we call the anagogical acts that so enkindle the heart.
105

Theological contemplation humanizes theology by making space for humility before the mystery of God. Resting in God's loving knowledge, assenting to it, allowing it to pierce the heart, sanctifies the present moment and constantly endows new eternal meaning to all the seemingly accidental particulars of one's life. If only contemporary theological reflection could be infused with this loving knowledge once again!

Only such a genuinely human theology can save and build up humanity. For 16th Century Spain, the rediscovery of this experience of the Lord rescued many Catholics from empty externalism and helped give birth to a more discerning Christian ethos which saw beyond much of the irrationality driving the rest of Europe. There is no lack of confidence in proclaiming the Gospel of Christ from the rooftops of society when people of faith root themselves in this living encounter with God. With such prayer imbued theology, the spiritual revolution witnessed in Denver can lead to the new evangelization of the modern metropolis so hoped for by Blessed John Paul II and Pope Benedict XVI.

God intends for us to find the space to be fully true to ourselves in this exchange of glances with Him, and once we find this space, He wills it to become our home, our dwelling place. Surely such a place is already the beginning of heaven. For those who want this beginning, St. John of the Cross repeats a maxim developed by the Carthusian Guigo II, "Seek in reading and you will find in meditation: knock in prayer and it will be opened to you in contemplation."106

This kind of knowing is a uniquely human moment, a vulnerable moment which progresses, or at least ought to progress, to

---

105 St. John of the Cross, *Sayings of Light and Love*, #139, *Complete Works*, 96.
106 *Sayings of Light and Love*, #158, *Complete Works*, 97. St. John of the Cross is citing Guigo's *Scala paradise*, chapter 2.

eternity. At the same time, the encounter of the Lord given in Sacred Doctrine is not an easy one. To meet the Lord in the depth of the heart is a moment of crisis where everything that betrays our humanity is revealed. In our next chapter we will see how the Lord helps us find the limits of our misery in the limitlessness of his mercy. In this difficult struggle, it is the glance of those loving eyes that prevent us from losing heart, eyes reflected in the doctrines we search.

Chapter Ten

Prayer and Mercy

We have come on a long journey together. In this pilgrimage of prayer, Christ first comes to us in our doubts and leads us to the mystery of the Cross. As we pass through this mystery, as we embrace it with our lives, we find ourselves encouraged by all kinds of messengers to seek Him, to take shelter in darkness, to stand firm in all kinds of battles, ascending a mysterious peak and entering into a secret place of intimate encounter. The friendship with God that unfolds in prayer is made fruitful in this encounter. God wants us to enjoy his friendship, but He also has a great and noble purpose for each of us.

Only as we spend time in prayer allowing Him to disclose His great love for us is He finally free to share with us this great purpose, this spiritual mission. What the great mission might be for any particular soul is such a beautiful and profound mystery that no book can possibly help one understand it. It is a reality between the soul and God, something He speaks deep in the substance of her being. In this chapter, we will look at one important facet of one's spiritual mission, the one dimension every spiritual mission shares in common – namely, in the name of the Father, Christ sends His disciples into the world in the power of the Holy Spirit to make known the mercies of God.

The humble movement of God's heart reaching out to ours, extending even into the deepest recesses of our misery, ought to evoke our love and gratitude. How often do we act with hostility instead? We feel a repugnance to the Lord. Something in us resists His advances. This is the nature of our misery.

We have already explored how the specific character of the lack of love in our hearts pertains to a rejection of God sewn into human nature. At the same time, this law of sin has neither completely corrupted us nor is it the deepest truth about our existence. What is good, noble and true about each of us is waiting to be set free. This is what Christ does for us. This is what we must do in His name for one another.

Those who come to realize what Christ suffered for their sakes yearn to give a return. They are so overcome by how much they are loved by Christ that they are willing to do anything for Him. They want to imitate Him in everything. We find this sentiment in the prayers and reflections of Blessed Charles de Foucauld who wanted to imitate in his own heart all the movements of the Heart of Jesus:

> My Father, I abandon myself into your hands. Make of me whatever pleases you. Whatever you do with me, I thank you: I am ready for all and I accept all. Only let your will be done in me and in all your creatures. I desire nothing else, my God. I place my soul in your hands, and I give it to you God with all the love of my heart, because I love you and I need to love, to give myself, to entrust myself into your hands without measure, with infinite confidence, because you are my Father.[107]

To make this movement in the Heart of Christ the movement of one's own heart is to allow oneself to be as rejected and hated as was the Lord Himself. When someone is really holy, primal hostility towards God in our culture and in the lives of individuals is directed at that person. This is the reason that Blessed Charles was betrayed to his murderers. It is the reason why great saints like Saint Maximilian Kolbe and Saint Teresa Benedicta of the Cross were killed in Auschwitz. It seems this is really the rea-

---

[107] *La Prière d'abandon,* January 23, 1897, translation my own.

son Blessed John Paul II was shot. It is also the reason he went into prison, embraced the man who shot him, and prayed with him.

If we want to follow the pilgrimage of prayer all the way to the end, we must not be frightened by the threats of the world. We have already seen how St. John of the Cross calls such worldly forces wild animals. They try to frighten the prayerful man or woman because these forces are frightened of the holiness of God. The trick to not succumbing to fear is to keep our eyes fixed on Jesus and His great love for us. This means we must search for His love everywhere, even in those places where it seems most absent. What does this mean? St. John of the Cross says "where there is no love, put love, and you will draw out love."[108]

It is in this radical availability to God that the Lord is achieving His greatest work: the perfection of His creation is the human person fully alive. Human beatitude is the ultimate purpose of God's creative and salvific act. Such beatitude is not brought about by rising above our frail humanity but by becoming more vulnerable human. To thrive, to really live to the fullest, one must become fully oneself, fully human.

Forgiveness and Beginning to Pray

One obstacle to beginning to pray and living within is the struggle to forgive. Whenever someone hurts us in a serious way, there is a spiritual wound that remains. As we begin to pray, it is common that we find ourselves going back over these wounds again and again. What is most frustrating is that many times we thought we had already forgiven the person who hurt us. But when the memory comes back, we can sometimes feel the anger and the pain all over again.

What do we do with the wounds so that they no longer impede our ability to pray? The *Catechism of the Catholic Church*

---

[108] See Letter 26, *Complete Works*, 760.

explains, "It is not in our power not to feel or to forget an offense; but the heart that offers itself to the Holy Spirit turns injury into compassion and purifies the memory in transforming hurt into intercession" (#2843).

Beginning to pray for those who have hurt us is difficult. In Scriptural terms, those who hurt us are our enemies, and this is true even when they are friends and close family members. Christ commands us to love our enemies and to do good to those who persecute us. Betrayal, abandonment, indifference, scandal, abuse, scorn, sarcasm, ridicule, detraction, and insult – these are all bitter things to forgive. The Lord grieves with us and for us when we suffer these things. He has permitted us to suffer them for a profound reason.

The Lord explained to his disciples that those who hunger and thirst for the sake of justice, those who are merciful, and especially those who are persecuted for righteousness and for the Lord, are blessed. Their mysterious beatitude only makes sense when we see through the eyes of faith the injustice and persecution they have endured. Somehow, trusting in God in the midst of such things makes them in the likeness of Christ. Trusting God means to pray for those who harm us, to seek to return good for evil. When this act of trust is made, the power of God is released in humanity. For two thousand years, this is what every martyr for our faith has revealed to the Church.

Why God Permits the Persecution of those He loves

In his mysterious wisdom and profound love, when the Father allows someone to hurt or oppose us in some way, He is entrusting that person to our prayers. When our enemy causes us to suffer unjustly, our faith tells us that this was allowed to happen so that we might participate in the mystery of the Cross. Somehow, like those who offered their lives for our faith, the mystery of redemption is being renewed through our own sufferings.

We have a special authority over the soul of someone who causes us great sorrow. Their actions have bound them to us in the mercy of God. Mercy is love that suffers the evil of another to affirm his dignity so that he does not have to suffer alone.[109] Whenever someone hurts us physically or even emotionally, he has demeaned himself even more. He is even more in need of mercy.

From this perspective, the injury our enemies have caused us can be a gateway for us to embrace the even greater sufferings with which their hearts are burdened. Because of this relationship, our prayers on their behalf have a particular power. The Father hears these prayers because prayer for our enemies enters deep into the mystery of the Cross. But how do we begin to pray for our enemies when the very thought of them and what they have done stirs our hearts with bitterness and resentment?

Here we must ask what it means to repent for our lack of mercy. The first step is the hardest. Whether they are living or dead, we need to forgive those who have hurt us. This is the hardest because forgiveness involves more than intellectually assenting to the fact that one ought to forgive.

We know that we get some pleasure out of our grievances. The irrational pleasure, we can sometimes take in these, distracts us from what God Himself desires us to do. What happens when all that pleasure is gone, when all we have left is the Cross? St. John of the Cross sees our poverty in the midst of great affliction as the greatest union possible with Christ Crucified in this life. To realize this solidarity with Christ, to cleave to his example with all of our strength, "When they are reduced to nothing, the highest degree of humility, the spiritual union between their souls and God will be an accomplished fact. This union is most noble and sublime state attainable in this life."[110]

---

[109] See *Summa Theologica* II-II, q.30, a.1
[110] *Ascent to Mt. Carmel*, book 2, chapter 7, 11, in *Complete Works*, 172.

To live by the Cross means choosing, over and over, whenever angry and resentful memories come up, not to hold a debt against someone who has hurt us. It means renouncing secret vows of revenge to which we have bound ourselves. It means not indulging in self-pity or in thinking ill of those who have sinned against us. It means begging God to show us the truth about our enemy's plight.

The Work of the Holy Spirit

Here, human effort alone cannot provide the healing such ongoing choices demand. Only the Lord's mercy can dissolve one's own hardness of heart toward those who have harmed us. We have to surrender our grievances to the Holy Spirit who turns "injury into compassion" and transforms "hurt into intercession."[111]

Like every Christian who has tried to follow Him, the Cross terrified Jesus. He sweat blood in the face of it. We believe that it was out of the most profound love for us and for His Father that He embraced this suffering. Because of this love, He would not have it any other way. Overcoming His own fear, He accepted death for our sake, and in accepting it, sanctified it so that it might become the pathway to new life.

Precisely because He has made death a pathway of life, Christians are also called to take up their crosses and follow Him. They must offer up resentment to God and allow their bitterness to die. Offering the gift of our grievances to God is especially pleasing to Him. It is part of our misery, and our misery is the only thing we really have to offer God that was not His to begin with.

This effort is spiritual, the work of the Holy Spirit. In order to forgive, we must pray, and sometimes we must devote many hours, days and even years to prayer for this purpose. It is a

---

[111] CCC 2849

difficult part of our *conversatio morum*. Yet we cannot dwell very deep in our hearts, we cannot live with ourselves if we do not find mercy for those who have offended us. *Habitare secum* is impossible without mercy.

There are moments in such prayer when we suddenly realize we must not only forgive, but we must ourselves ask for forgiveness. A transformation takes place where our attention shifts from the evil done to us to the plight of the person who inflicted it. Every time we submit resentment to the Lord, every time we renounce a vengeful thought, every time we offer the Lord the deep pain in our heart, even if we do not feel or understand it, we have made room for the gentle action of the Holy Spirit.

The Holy Spirit does not take the wounds away. They remain like the wounds in the hands and side of Christ. The wounds of Christ are a pathway into the heart of every man and woman. This is because the hostility of each one of us towards Him caused those wounds. Similarly when someone wounds us, the wound can become a pathway into that person's heart. Wounds bind us to those who have hurt us, especially those who have become our enemies, because whenever someone hurts us, he has allowed us to share in his misery, to know the lack of love he suffers. With the Holy Spirit, this knowledge is a powerful gift.

Once the Holy Spirit shows us this truth, we have a choice. We can choose to suffer this misery with the one who hurt us in prayer so that God might restore their dignity. When we choose this, our wounds like the wounds of Christ no longer dehumanize as long as we do not backslide. Instead, the Holy Spirit transforms such wounds into founts of grace. Those who have experienced this will tell you, with the grace of Christ, there is no room for bitterness. There is only great compassion and sober prayerfulness.

St. Thomas Aquinas on Mercy and the Gift of Counsel

As we go further into the discussion of St. Thomas Aquinas on mercy, he explains that the Holy Spirit's gift of counsel is a special prompting, or impetus, in the heart that brings every act of mercy to perfection.[112] The gift of counsel, explains St. Thomas, allows us to know and to understand the misery in the hearts of others. Once we know and understand their misery, we can bind ourselves to them in prayer so that those who have hurt us might feel the mercy of God in their misery; and this that they might find a reason to hope, a pathway out of the hell in which they are imprisoned.

It is by this same gift that Christ knew our hostility to God and allowed Himself to be wounded unto death by it. He wanted to bear this dehumanizing force in our nature that it might die with Him. This way, when He rose again, He could free from futility all that is most good, noble and true about each of us.

Likewise with us, this same gift allows us to extend Christ's saving work into the hearts of others. In particular, the gift of counsel allows us to understand the dehumanizing hostility others have unleashed on us and by understanding it in faith, to offer it to God in love. When we do this, our mercy perfected by the Holy Spirit makes space in the hearts of those who have hurt us, space into which God's love can flow. It is the saving mercy of God, His love suffering our misery, which is the only hope for humanity.

---

[112] See *Summa Theologica* II-II, q.30, a. 1 and q.52, a.4.

CONCLUSION:
Forsake not the Discipline

These last words of St. Anthony of the Desert are a gentle admonishment to all who would climb the hidden mountain and enter the secret garden of prayer. Anthony Bloom's *Beginning to Pray* was inspired at least in part by his patron, St. Anthony of the Desert. St. Anthony taught that no matter how far we progress, we are always beginners. According to him, we must never look back on past accomplishments, but instead each day we must be disciplined in making a new fresh start in our devotion to the Lord.

Our devotion to Jesus Christ is renewed whenever we take up this discipline, whenever we begin to pray. Always this beginning seems so fragile. We are so inconstant, so easily swayed this way and that, so easily distracted. So often we discover that we have lost our way, fallen into a trap and forgotten to turn to the Lord. So many mistakes are made from the outset and often these mistakes lead to great confusion. Some even give up altogether. When this happens, we must not lose heart. It is time for us to begin again. This present work represents a humble attempt to help those who have given up, or feel on the verge on doing so, to make this new beginning.

A Love Stronger than Death

Blessed John Paul II was constant in the discipline of prayer, the discipline of beginning each day as the Lord entrusted him with greater and greater pastoral responsibilities. He would dedicate the first hours of every morning to Mass and silent prayer.

176

He prayed ardently and with great confidence in the face of situations which seemed humanly impossible to solve. His being a catalyst for helping to change political realities was only possible because of his intense prayer life.

Prayer is a cry of the heart to the Father that His Will might be done. Anyone can wish this on a sentimental level. To really learn to desire what God desires, to really know what to ask for and how, this can only be learned when we follow Christ crucified from Gethsemane to Calvary. The wisdom of prayer is learned at the price of great suffering. For the Christian must also learn how "if it is Your Will let this cup pass" becomes "into Your Hand I commend my spirit."

Without entering into Christ's passion and death, prayer remains merely a nice thought, a polite thing to say to the Lord or at least for others to hear. Suffering, trials, vigilance and the feeling of abandonment – these are the things of love that not only test us, but attract God. Trials expose our powerlessness and move us to trust God more deeply. It is precisely at this moment that we can make of our prayers something beautiful for God, something worthy of His hearing. Such prayers make space for God to act. When a difficult trial occasions this kind of trust, our prayer finally becomes Christ-like.

Christ-like prayer yearns for all He yearns for, and this yearning evokes petitions for things so deeply desired and so little understood that sometimes no words can be found for them. One finds oneself moaning in prayer, crying tears of compunction, if not for oneself, for the general brokenness of the world.

This in fact is how John Paul II prayed. He prayed from the depths of his heart with great intensity. He sighed, he groaned, he wept. Sometimes, his whole body would shake. His prayers were ardent. What trials were driving him to pray like Christ? I can only guess. Having guided his flock through difficult years as the Archbishop of Krakow, when he became pope he already understood the fear and lack of confidence that had

177

gripped the Church. I believe it was his concern for those entrusted to his care that drove him to ardent prayer.

After all the murder and destruction inflicted on Europe, through the oppression imposed by ideological misunderstandings of the human person, and in the midst of starving and persecuted Christian populations around the world, it seemed everyone was shaken. Many were asking, at least interiorly, whether our patrimony of prayer was still relevant, whether any of it was really real.

Thinkers, like Hans Urs von Balthasar, discerned that the Church was suffering through a historical and cultural kind of Holy Saturday. Applying Jesus' words to St. Faustina we saw earlier, whole societies were treating God as if He were dead. In America, and other First World countries in particular, not only were priests and religious forsaking the solemn promises to God, but married couples had bought into a contraceptive mentality to the point of forsaking their children, and one another, in easy no-fault divorce.

The Church needed a word of hope. Confidence in the Gospel of Christ needed to be restored. On the day of his election, Blessed John Paul II could not have possibly known that his whole pontificate would be defined by the first words he spoke as Pope "Be not afraid...Open wide the doors to Christ."

His pastoral efforts centered around preparing the World for the Third Millennium of Christianity by leading the Church to fully celebrate the Great Jubilee of the Year 2000. World Youth Days, including the one held in Denver with which we started our exploration, were part of this preparation. He understood that the youth made present the hope of the Church. It was their gift to the body of Christ.

This means their role was not reserved for some distant moment. They needed to bring the gift of hope they already possessed to bear in the life of the Church in the concrete, present moment we live in now. The Church, the Pope and God were counting on them.

Their witness and enthusiasm was to be the great instrument by which the loving Presence of the Risen Christ would be made known to those who had lost their confidence and would help the whole Church continue its pilgrimage in the 21st Century. All of this was realized in remarkable ways throughout the celebrations of the Year 2000.

Then, all of the wonderful joy of the Jubilee seemed to be crushed in the years that followed. The senseless murder of thousands of innocent people perpetrated on September 11, 2001, the decimation of Christian populations in Islamic countries, whole waves of brutal genocide, horrific scandal after horrific scandal sowing distrust of the priesthood, all kinds of serious failures in leadership by the bishops, and unrelenting media attacks on all aspects of the Church, including the sacred institution of marriage by gleeful politicians, lawyers and news reporters—some of whom were themselves Catholic. In the midst of this, worn out by both his disease and his service to the Lord, Blessed John Paul II died a very difficult death.

Why does God want us to pray? There is a temptation to think that prayer is superfluous. He is all knowing and all powerful. He already knows what we want before we ask. When we do ask it often seems to accomplish nothing at all.

Yet He will not act until we ask Him to. The reason He will only act if we ask Him is that prayer is an essential part in His eternal plan that He entrusted to man and woman at the dawn of our creation. He has placed His trust in us, confident that we will freely choose to fulfill what He has desired for us from before the foundation of the world.

Here we get to a truth that is very difficult to explain, but must be addressed. Everyone assumes that a great saint is someone who is above the fray, invulnerable to the plight of the rest of humanity. But it is really quite the opposite. The more we pray, the more vulnerable we become.

Blessed John Paul II in the days before his death pulled himself up to his window and peeked out at the crowds of young people who were praying for him in St. Peter's Square. Sick and weak as he was the presence of young people always gave him new strength. But that day, after recalling his many visits to young people around the world, he thanked them for coming to pray for him, "I have sought you out and now you come to me … thank you."

His words were from the heart. The presence of the young people and other pilgrims, their witness together in prayer, was a great consolation to him. In the face of all kinds of evil over which he could not help but be concerned, they were a great sign the Lord had heard his prayer. They shared together a solidarity in the Lord because they with him were not afraid to open wide the doors to Christ.

The Role of Mary in the Life of Prayer

John Paul II discovered the secret of making a new beginning daily as a young man in Krakow just at the time of the Nazi invasion. His parish was administered by Salesian priests who knew that their days were numbered. In fact, many Polish priests would be interned in concentration camps during the war, and a significant number of these would die in the midst of the most brutal conditions. The Salesians prepared for this eventuality by asking a layman to form a prayer group of young people who would be trained in the spiritual life and catechesis. The prayer group was called the "Living Rosary." Each member would form his own "Living Rosary" group so that when the priests were imprisoned the faith could continue.

The layman whom they tapped was a tailor noted for his deep prayer and knowledge of Saint John of the Cross. Jan Tyronowski had chosen his life of solitude and his humble occupation because it provided him the silence he needed to enter into deep prayer. At the same time, though he was simple, he was not a simpleton. Rather, he was an intellectual whose understanding of spiritual theology introduced the young people entrusted to him to deep truths regarding the human person and the nature of faith. Blessed John Paul II's approach in his doctoral studies on St. John of the Cross suggests an originality which might have been born in the catechesis providing through Tyronoski's "Living Rosary" catechesis.

Besides the Carmelite doctrine on prayer and spiritual growth, which much of this book has been dedicated to, another important part of the catechesis Tyronowski offered in the spiritual life is the maternal role of Mary in the life of prayer. Because of her unique relationship with Christ, she has a special role to play in the spiritual life of each believer. Her prayer for us helps us in our efforts to pray. Tyronowski was an advocate that those who love Jesus should take his Mother into their homes.

Liturgically, at the end of the last hour of the liturgical day, Night Prayer, the Church commends everything to the intercession of the Virgin Mary. She is a special protection through the night until the new day. So to as we come to the end of this work do we commend ourselves to the Mother of the Lord who is solicitous that we should always, "Go and do whatever He tells you."

Marian Consecration

John Paul II would eventually consecrate himself to Mary according to the form proposed by St. Louis de Montfort, a great mystic whose teaching is deeply rooted in what many call the "French School" of spirituality. Key to this teaching is that growth in holiness is realized through total identification with Jesus through Mary. The future pope seems to have always understood that all authentic devotion to Mary leads to deeper union with Jesus. Scripturally, after all, she is the one who commands that we do whatever He tells us. What he came to be astonished by was the fact that Jesus entrusts His Mother to those who dedicate themselves to prayer. His encyclical *Mother of the Redeemer* includes an important explanation of this mystical reality in the context of Golgatha.

The Scriptures explain to us that Mary stood at the foot of the Cross with the Beloved Disciple. John Paul II observes that throughout the life of Jesus one can observe what seems to be a peculiar distancing. Jesus up to that moment does not express the normal affection that one might expect the Lord to have for His Mother.

At the same time, we must interpret His words and actions concerning His Mother in relation to her obedience to the Father from the first moment He was conceived and to her radical following of Him to the Cross. The Lord's mysterious way of relating with Mary reveals that his new creation of all of us was already beginning in her. By His grace, Jesus shows His power to re-create woman; making Mary, the New Eve.

At the Wedding Feast of Cana, the Lord seems to reject her when He addresses her as "woman," but her reaction is like a queen mother whose request the King cannot reject.[113]   Later, when someone exclaims that the womb that bore Him and the breasts that fed Him were blessed, the Word of the Father counters by declaring that those are blessed rather who hear His word and keep it.[114] Again, when someone informs Him that His mother and brothers are outside, the Son of God declares that only those who do the will of the Father are mother and brothers to Him.[115]   Each apparent rejection is actually an affirmation: the woman Mary, the New Eve, is the one who hears and keeps His word, and she is His Mother precisely because of her radical obe-

---

[113] See John 2:3-5.
[114] See Luke 8:19-21
[115] See Luke 11:27-28.

dience of the will of the Father. Such is the power of the grace of Christ that it can reconstitute our humanity to conform to the truth He reveals.

The sign of God's mysterious love Mary provides throughout the ministry of Christ reaches its climax at the foot of the Cross. As at the Wedding Feast of Cana, Jesus looking at his Mother, calls her "Woman." And then, He gives her to the disciple whom He loved. This Beloved Disciple likewise takes her into his "home." [116]

This act of entrustment whereby Jesus gives His Mother to the disciple whom He loves speaks to a very special grace offered to those who strive to begin to pray. Jesus offers each of us His Mother, and if we choose to take her into our hearts, choose to welcome her into our lives, she offers us the same maternal affection she offered Jesus. By accepting the gift of Mary, we make ourselves, in a spiritual sense, her sons and daughters.

It is to this end that a tradition arose in the Catholic patrimony of prayer of consecrating oneself to Jesus through Mary. Sometimes called Marian Consecration, this spiritual act of welcoming Mary into one's life and entrusting her with everything allows her to entrust to us everything in her maternal heart: the fruit of the most profound contemplation of her Son and the Work of redemption. Such an exchange of hearts between the Mother of the Lord and a disciple who welcomes her expands the life of prayer, so that our efforts to pray are infused with the prayers of the Virgin Mother.

Redeemed by the sacrifice of her Son on the Cross, Mary's natural motherhood has been transformed by His Blood into a spiritual motherhood. She prays for every Christian that the gift of faith might be nurtured and come to maturity. For those who welcome this maternal mediation of the grace of Christ into their hearts, she is able to lead them into the same obedient faith by

---

[116] See John 19:26-27 and Blessed John Paul II in *Redemptoris Mater*, ##20-24.

which she too followed her Son to the Cross to participate in His work of redemption.

Blessed Elisabeth of the Trinity understood this in a beautiful way. She reflects on the unique knowledge that Mary had of her Son, not only because she was His mother, but most of all because she accompanied her Son with faith from His conception all the way to His Crucifixion, pondering all these things in her heart.[117] Mary contemplated Jesus' obedience on the Cross more profoundly than any other human being.

This obedience, according to Blessed Elisabeth, was a great song of praise. Because Mary carries this song of praise in her heart, she can teach it to those who entrust themselves to her intercession. Because of this, in those painful crucifying moments of our lives, if we ask Mary, she will help us offer the same song of praise that Jesus offered on the Cross magnifying His glory and extending the work of redemption to the world by making up in our own bodies "what is lacking in the suffering of Christ" and with our lives offering true "spiritual worship."

Throughout these pages on beginning to pray, I have tried to explain how the hidden mountain and secret garden of prayer is a connection, a bridge to eternal life in heaven. For those who welcome Mary and allow her to teach them the Heart of her Son, they come to know Mary as Elisabeth of the Trinity did. For Elisabeth and for all such disciples, Mary becomes for them *Janua Coeli*, the Gate of Heaven.

Blessed John Paul II lived out his intimacy with Christ Jesus by entrusting his life of prayer into the maternal hands of Mary. His motto, *Totus Tuus* (Wholly Yours) refers to this special relationship. She who obediently followed the Lord, who allowed herself to be raised in the order of grace from a natural motherhood to a supernatural motherhood, accompanies all those who allow themselves to be raised up by her Son into the new existence of grace which Christian prayer makes possible. Those who

---

[117] See *Last Retreat*, ##40-41.

will welcome Mary into their hearts will soon find themselves a vital part of the spiritual revolution initiated under John Paul II's leadership, a revolution that has already begun to change the world in which we live.

Our Spiritual Home

As his last days approached, Blessed John Paul II expressed his desire to go to the Father's house. In his heart, he already knew that the Father's house was his true home. Home is a place of communion and friendship. It is permeated with the peace and joy that is only found in loving those entrusted to us, and even more in knowing that we are loved. In this life and in this world, we are never really at home. We are never fully at peace. Our joy is never quite what it ought to be. Deep inside we know we are made for another kind of existence.

Our heavenly homeland, the spiritual household to which we belong, is the bosom of the Trinity. The God of Christianity is not a pantheistic power into which personal uniqueness is absorbed. Nor is our God some nihilistic void into which all identity and personality is annihilated. Through Christ, through identifying ourselves with His work of redemption, we draw ever closer to the heart of the Trinity to become more fully human.

This paradox reveals the beautiful mystery of our life in Christ: we discover the truth about our humanity by giving ourselves in love for one another as He did for us. The more completely we conform our lives to Christ crucified by offering our earthly existence to God, the more the unique and unrepeatable gift God made us to be is revealed to ourselves and to the world. This gift of self by grace makes possible all kinds of relations of genuine love, a living communion in which all that is most noble and good about humanity can thrive. The Father's house, into which Jesus invites us, is a society that is discovered not only at the end of our days, but right now, in the present moment, in time, which Elisabeth explains is "eternity begun and still in progress."[118]

To come home, to be welcomed at last in our true home, this is a primordial prayer that yearns for fulfillment. This is because the desire for friendship, communion and being together is a reality of the heart – not only in the hearts of women and men, but also in the heart of God. Whenever anyone realizes this desire, even if for only the briefest of moments, that individual tastes life to the full; the very life that Christ came to give. What is more, the home we yearn for is not in some distant place that is difficult to get to. Our home is with the Lord, and the Lord dwells in our hearts. To find him, we merely need to begin to seek his presence within for "the Kingdom of God is within you."[119]

Now is the Time:
Seek the Hidden Mountain and Secret Garden of Prayer

Climbing the hidden mountain and entering the secret garden of prayer is our journey to the One whose coming is certain and whose Kingdom is without end. This journey crosses the bridge of His Crucified Body and enters into the embrace of the Father in the power of the Holy Spirit. Even if it starts with doubt and hostility, prayer is a pursuit of lovers, divine and human, one for the other, through all kinds of darkness, trials and death. Such prayer journeys by the night of faith and takes up a battle against irrationality. Prayer ascends a mountain to which only the Lord can lead us. It descends into the abyss of the heart and finds a garden of love. Prayer progresses to our true home, to a day that will have no end: this is the greatness of prayer which faith in Christ opens up.

We have shared together some of the insights that are firing up a whole new generation of young men and women ready

---

[118] *Heaven in Faith*, #1
[119] Luke 17:21.

to climb the Lord's mountain and eager to enter the garden of His love. They want to serve the Bridegroom for whose coming they yearn. They are neither enchanted by the empty promises of pop-culture nor afraid of the heartless brutality it incubates. They see God's love, not moral failure, as the defining characteristic of humanity. Captivated by the One whom they have set out to find, they are dedicated to helping the world welcome Him with joy.

The decision to do something beautiful for God binds these young people together in friendship. Often misunderstood, even by those close to them, they have given up everything to serve their Crucified Master. Enduring daily trials, hardships and challenges, they have found an unshakable foundation in the Risen Lord through prayer. Their fruitfulness is testimony to the power of Christ Jesus and the spiritual revolution started under the leadership of John Paul II.

If your heart is drawn to the hidden mountain and secret garden, now is the time; this is the hour. Do not delay. Do not be afraid. As Blessed John Paul II exhorted us, "Be proud of the Gospel of Christ. Shout it from the rooftops!"

A spiritual revolution has begun and the Lord himself is inviting you make this journey and to join His cause. The blessings He has predestined you to share are irreplaceable in the divine calling we have together during the brief span of our earthly lives: the vocation to build a culture of life and a civilization of love, a place in which the genuinely human will thrive—where the glory of God is man fully alive.

About the Author

Dr. Anthony Lynn Lilles is a graduate of Franciscan University of Steubenville, and completed his graduate and postgraduate studies at the *Angelicum*. He has worked in Northern Colorado for over twenty years in various parishes and the Office of Liturgy for the Archdiocese of Denver. After having served as Academic Dean of St. John Vianney Theological Seminary, he is currently an associate professor of theology. Most of his research has been devoted to the spiritual doctrine of Blessed Elisabeth of the Trinity O.C.D. and the Carmelite Doctors of the Church. A married father of three, he is grateful to God for his family and for the life they share at the foot of the Rocky Mountains.

About the Publisher

Discerning Hearts is an official not for profit 501 (c)(3) apostolate based in Omaha, Nebraska. Its mission responds to the Church's call to use the media for evangelization, catechesis and spiritual renewal.

"Discerning Hearts is a trusted resource for Catholic spirituality and teaching. I support it as an apostolate for the new evangelization that brings the Good News to every corner of the world through the internet."
- Most Reverend George J. Lucas, Archbishop of Omaha

For more information visit www.discerninghearts.com

Title
Imitating Mary

Book - Mary - Dunlau..com

Author — by March Femalew -
B. Benalawn
Fenalang

Marge Fenelel

Made in the USA
San Bernardino, CA
22 February 2013